Selected Poems

by

Hazel Archard

Biography

Hazel Archard (née Thorpe) was born in Eastbourne on 1st June 1920 the youngest in a close knit family. She was educated at Eastbourne High School and graduated in French and German at London University. She taught during the war years and for some while after, at Lewes County Grammar School for Boys. She then taught at Eastbourne High School until giving up teaching to look after her husband's elderly aunt. She met her future husband James Archard, a small farmer farming at Piltdown Sussex at the Lewes Little Theatre. They had a long and loving marriage, until only a few months after their golden wedding anniversary she had a first and massive stroke and died without regaining consciousness in November 1996. She was one of the Downland Poets' Group in Eastbourne, a member of the Labour Party, of Friends of the Earth and the Campaign for Nuclear Disarmament. She spent many nights camping at Greenham, the American nuclear base.

All her life she enjoyed writing, but especially poetry.

First Published in Great Britain in 1998 by Moses Farm Publications, Piltdown, East Sussex

A Catalogue copy for this book is available from the British Library
ISBN 0 9531978 08

Typesetting, layout and printing by Small Print, The Malthouse, Llangollen. Wales Tel: +44 (0)1978 861990

Acknowledgements

Some of these poems have previously appeared elsewhere and acknowledgements are due to the editors, publishers and others concerned.

Dawn in a Garden and *Long Wind* in *The Field.*
Hunger Eats the Seed in Poetry Now.
Lone Creature by Arrival Press
Panic Pipe by Anchor Press
Housebound with *Poetry on the Buses* promoted by S E Arts,
The Dormouse (Glis) in *Hear my Story* JC/MC books
Confrontation in *Lateral Moves 1997*
The following first published by *New Statesman:*
The Clock, Martello, On Women, White Eagle and *Sunday*
Poems first published in A View from the Field are marked with an asterisk in Contents.
The Rock Housman Society Poetry Competition Anthology, 1997-1998.

James Archard wishes to thank Maud Rix, Eileen Boniface, and Ali Saddighzadeh for their help in preparing this publication and Martin Spencer for his portrait of the author and for the drawing.

Contents

*First published in A View from the Field

Wandering into Love

When first I heard your voice and saw your face
There fell no shaft of lightning from above,
Nor did I fall, but wandered into love
As walking in a rare enchanted space.

And as I wandered, at a halting pace,
There came a warmth, not to the heart alone
But in the very marrow of the bone.
That soft suffusion, bearing up its trace

Behind my vision, made this earthly place
Intense in colour; flowers grew in size;
The sombre city smiled into my eyes,
And to be living was an act of grace.

Then, as those ardent eyes were helped to see,
They saw with joy you were in love with me.

Sunday

The milk arrives, the papers come; there isn't any post;
The morning, for an English Mum, turns on the Sunday roast;
While visiting aunts go off to church and vicars call the banns,
And Fathers polish up the car and the kids walk down to Gran's
And much of Monday's wash goes out, and dinner's after one,
And somebody else but Mother goes and gets the dishes done.
The city spills, the country fills, how *Sunday* looks the sea!
Fresh cakes are made, a clean cloth laid, the boyfriend comes to tea.
And after seven, spades hang up and mowers roll away,
And wheeling flocks in cycling socks are bound to get home today.
And dusk comes down on weary lines that crawl in from the coast,
And Monday breathes in the larder cold, congealing the Sunday roast.

Another Sea

High on the cliff-top where the Downland breaks
        The calm turf makes
        A brim of green.
    The sunken sea that lies below
    Has never seen and cannot tell
    How wide and far the Downlands go
    In surging sweep, in rolling swell,
    The billows deep yet smooth, serene,
The turf so green in undulating flow:
Wide waters, heaving under stony spell.
    Only the languid rivers glean
    Some notion as they drift between,
And the waves murmur underneath the cliff,
    Wondering if . . .
But there the flowing rock stands sheer and stiff.

Beaver, Less Eager

Sit me on the nearest sofa.
Let me play the idle loafer.
Bread to eat and beer to drink,
Now's the time to stop and think.
Eager beaver, busy beaving,
Are your objects worth achieving?
Have you thought, for all your damming,
Flowing water's not for jamming?
All that heaving! All that biting!
Have you got it down in writing
That to bar the final sluice
Any dam will be of use?
Shall I sweat for house and car,
Villa, boat and cocktail bar
Or be happy kipping here
Damming up a pint of beer?

Bearing Gift

Cry for the moon by night
- Small fading scar -
But never set your sight
        On any star
That points the unreflecting sky:
        A sight too high,
        A cry too far.
Few men are wise, but if they were
        Kings would confer
No gold, no incense; only myrrh:
With myrrh you know just where you are.

Green Lane

Now all the lane is greeny grass
        - Forgotten time ago -
And carts and cattle rut the way
        While Rathmin roses blow
On hedges high with haw and hip,
With blackberry and sloe;
A sunny scene, where youth is green,
And dallies down, the fields between,
And lads are leading lasses on
        As far as they will go,
With a hey! and a nonny, nonny!
        Which is not so sharp as no!
- Yet look: this lane is hedged along
        With houses in a row.
They call it Green. What can they mean?
I like to think it may have been,
        But cannot find it so.

Bee on a Pane

Heavy with scented sweetness for the comb
    He lurches home,
Full-freighted as a continental truck,
And hums along, still musing in his cups:
    Those petalled calyces
    Beloved of honey bees.
The carriageway seems clear, but now it ups
    - Congealed in sudden freeze -
And hits him on the nose. Ah, just his luck
To find a summer-house with open door
And have no sense to back! Bowed to the knees,
He climbs the vertical, stays in a corner, stuck,
    Stopped dead,
- Though all the road lies visible ahead -
High revving with frustrated engine roar;
Until a god leans out of his machine,
    Happy to intervene,
And moves the frozen air to open breeze.

Blood Moon

Gibbous as a golden quince
Hanging bright and hard and yellow,
Hunter's moon came slowly round,
Hung about a hunting ground,
Ripening in October.
Came a bowman, loony fellow,
    More than mellow,
    Scarcely sober,
Thought it game to please a prince,
Shot the sitting moon. It bled.
Hunter's moon has ever since
    Risen red.

Begging the Question

He begged the question not to go away:
It was a good one, relevant and sound,
And better treated fully, later in the day.
But when the question tried again it found
The cunning beggar hadn't time to stay.

History

The proving finger writes, and having writ,
Proves on. But don't believe a word of it.

Monkey with the Atom Bomb

As we commemorate the dead,
By Cenotaph and grave
The hapless and the brave,
Both enemy and friend
I hear the cynic in my head
Saying as it has always said:
The wars will never end.
Fighting forward, fighting back,
We humans bloodily attack
And bloodily defend.

The arrow's head, the blunderbuss,
Lethal gas and rapid bullet
- Got a trigger, gotta pull it -
These have not extinguished us.
Monkey with the atom bomb:
See our Armageddon come.
That would be our just deserts.
- Very sorry if it hurts -

Dreamspiders

Now, take the money spider - (find your own,
Leave mine alone) -
Divide it with your cerebral dividers
Into a million mites; and here be spiders
(Actual size)
Who craft the dreams behind our sleeping eyes.
Deep in the myriad chambers of the mind
They snare the thoughts that consciousness forgets
And all day long, on silken spinnerets,
They thread and wind
The stuff of dreams, and work it into webs
Hung with the dew of sleep. When daylight ebbs
In hollows of the head they hang their nets,
Shaking out slumber-drops to paralyse
The watchful motions of our heavy eyes.
As night must fall, so droops the outer lid,
Then all is hid.

What if a waking flash light up the brain?
They snatch their skein
And in the twinkling of an inward eye
They scuttle up to secret cells on high.
But certain little spinners, half asleep,
Lost in the leap,
On wafted webs come drifting down again.
Then dreams are plain.
Or sometimes, as a mischievous delight
A wispy trail of dying dream is shed.
Then lurking spinners whisk away the thread
And a dream vanishes in darkest night.

Child in Age

All through the livelong day
I pulled each pointed hour,
Bright petals from a daisy flower
Of radiant display.
But where those scattered petals went
Now that my time is shrivel-spent
Is more than I can say.
Forgotten flowers are grey.
Sleepily staring, here I sit
And wonder what to make of it
All through the die-long day.

Sonnet for the Day

New every morning, when the welkin rings
With wild alarum shrilling by the bed,
From groping round to hit it on the head
We shudder down, protesting with the springs.

Too soon, when seeping early light has spread
A surface over old familiar things,
Beyond the blinded pane a song-bird sings:
High call that fills a lowly earth with dread.

For some must die that others may be fed.
The worm turns out, while death waits in the wings.
Such is the pattern each new morning brings.
And now the crumpled cares of night are fled

To lurk in sneaking ambush through the day.
We must be off, then, to be on their way.

Day of the Binder

It was no easy life, those ways
Of harvesting, in younger days.
First, opening the field up with a scythe.
A man did that, in sweat, though strong and lithe,
Clearing the first run round the crop.
Then came the binder, started up, to stop:
- The twine not tying fast, or the knife jammed -
But drew away more rhythmically, slammed
Each sheaf aside: long bundles, heavy, stout.
We worked towards the middle, carving out
Long curving corners where the tractor turned
To pull back in. It was a knack you learned.
A neighbour waited, patient, with a gun
To see a rabbit run
As the last sweep cut off his long retreat.
A swig of cooling drink, and on your feet
Setting the stooks up while the heads were dry,
And keeping cocked an anxious weather eye.
Stout sheaf beneath each arm, you had to thwack
Two heads together, build a triple rack,
Stalks in the stubble, wind to dry the crown.
But gales blew up to blow them down
And brought the rain to soak them on the ground.
We stood them up again, and turned them round.
Some years the ears began to sprout.
We pulled them out.
Later than soon, the weather willed
We should bring home what was not spoilt or spilled
Up to the stackyard. So the several fields
Gave up their wrested yields.
Out came the wagons, and a trailer, low,
- Easier loading - not so high to throw.
Up went the pitchforked sheaves: another knack
Which nearly broke your back.
A woman built the load, reaching for sheaves,

And coming out a bit more on the eaves,
Then binding in, and catching rope to swarm
Down at the other end, all scratched and warm,
Sweating. But sometimes one would ride,
    Flattened, exhausted, high,
Aboard the laden wagon, staring at a sky
    Which rocked from side to side.

Bonfires

They lit a bonfire up on Beacon Hill
When plundering marauders came to kill.
It spread a terror over all the shire.
When Fawkes is guyed, on piles of burning tyre,
The children's shrieks sound all too shrill.
But wafted pale across the autumn sun,
Thin smoke of crackled leaves and sticks on fire
And tongues of flame leaping to heart's desire,
    That makes a bonfire fun.

Dance of the Dusk

Dusk gathers with the midges as they fall
    And rise
And fall and daze the eyes
    Of drowsy day,
Threading a gauzy hay
    A hazy pall
Till dark comes deeply down and swallows all.

Cheeseparing

A story on our reading list
Told of a German chauvinist
Who chose the handmaid of his life
By handing her a kitchen knife,
Some rinded cheese, and saying, 'Cut it'
The first one did her darnedest, but it
Availed her not: the rind too thick.
The next contender ran up quick
But pared the rind a mite too fine.
'Disqualified! You can't be mine'
The third used all her Hausfraunous
And cut it right. She keeps his house.
This way of wooing's sure to please
But comes expensive on the cheese.

The Eye of a Needle

A camel looked a needle in the eye
And saw that it was very small indeed.
Ridiculous! I wouldn't even try,
And luckily I've never felt the need.
Yet proud I am to symbolise
A monster of enormous size,
In heaven's view ungainly - human greed.

Said the needle to the thimble,
He can call himself a symbol,
But these parables are tricky things to read,
For modern commentators state
- (It's all my eye) -that I'm a gate,
Yet if I prick a rich man he will bleed.

I Blame all those Scientists

In days of yore
And long before
Whatever yore might be
The sun rose high
To light the sky
For them and you and me.
We watched and prayed;
All day it stayed,
And went down after tea.

The earth was flat
As brim of hat
(With here and there a hill)
And if a ship
Poured over lip,
That was the Father's will.
And that was that,
While earth just sat
And kept serenely still.

Our shifting ground
Now rushes round
Itself and round the sun,
With poor old Man
An also-ran
Whose race is early run.
If we are not
The central clot
In any Milky Way,
Pray tell me why
The blazes I
Should rise and shine today.

The Dormouse (Glis)

(A True Winter's Tale)

We took the topmost bale of straw,
But cuddled on the next we saw
A little sleeping mouse,
About an inch from head to tail,
A strawy colour, like the bale
He made his winter house.
And there he lay, and did not stir,
A wispy little tuft of fur,
A helpless little hummock,
His breath so still he might be dead
His tail curled up around his head
Which lay upon his stomach.
Enormous autumn appetite
Had stuffed this pillow ticking-tight
Before he hibernated,
But now, with winter nearly past,
Because of his protracted fast
His stomach was deflated.
So there he lay, all thin and pale
And small, and vulnerably frail;
And yet, to me it seems
A life of bliss for dormouse (Glis)
To sleep all winter snug as this,
Emerging in a kindly spring
To gorge himself like anything
Till bursting at the seams.
We put the straw bale gently back,
Then chose another from the stack
And left him to his dreams.

Daisies and Buttercups

Daisies and buttercups beguiled
The fickle fancy of a child.
All white and golden on the green
They lighted up the summer scene
    With brightness from below.
The daisy flowers on threaded stems
Made bracelets, garlands, diadems;
A buttercup beneath the chin
Shed soft reflection on the skin,
    But that was long ago.

A sweep of green sets off the border;
Common weeds are out of order.
    So it came to pass
    My heart went out to grass.
Every daisy-clustered shoot
    - I have it by the root,
And as for golden buttercup,
    I dig it up.
How can I ever make amends
For such inconstancy to friends?
Soon time will tell, the story ends
When nature gives her bounteous pardon
To gardeners grown too old to garden.
There as I sit and snooze and slack
Old friends will soon come trooping back
And I shall settle to be lazy
With golden buttercup and daisy.

Bird Watcher

The robin hops for my delight,
A favour which I well requite
When hoeing in his patch.
Although I'm master of his sod
He does not rank me as a god
Because I cannot match
His notion of the Bird above
Whom all good robins learn to love.
I'm from a faulty batch
Which cannot creditably sing,
Which grows no feathers on its wing,
Which sets no eggs to hatch.
Yet, as I find him grubs and worms,
I gain acceptance on his terms
As one brought up to scratch.

Common Place

Our common is a common one,
Not in the least de luxe,
Where dogs take people for a run
And people feed the ducks.
The tread-bare paths that wind about
Hold puddles in the dust,
The iron seats, made firm and stout,
Are weathering to rust.
Yet now the may is coming out
We're almost upper -crust!
Our gorse is in its glory now,
Our parsley-lace is fine,
Crab-apple blossom hides the bough,
The dandelions shine.
I feel some pride, reflecting how
This place is yours and mine.

Cornish Coast

Swept by the seas on either hand,
    The craggy Cornish coast
Is battered by the running tide
    As first and furthermost.
Hard cliffs, which like a bastion stand
To turn the storming surf away,
Invite the waters just inside
With creek and cove and basking bay,
To glimpse a green and golden land:
High-roosting roof tops, perching streets,
Spring-flowered meadows, wooded streams,
Gay-painted ports and fishing fleets,
Sanctified springs and sunken seams
    With their abandoned ghost.
Here, where the air is tempered warm
By wind and water's clemency,
The last of land extends its arm
To welcome the approaching sea.
    - A genial, friendly host.

Fellow Travellers

Hark how the wind is torn
    Shrieking through thorn
And moaning under lash of branches bare,
    Hauled by the hair,
On into emptiness continually borne.
Pity the wind, all you who start from sleep,
    Fearful, to listen. Share
With anguish in the shuddering of air.
Leave it some cranny open, let it creep
To shelter sighing on the darkened stair.

Naked River Bather

Along a sunny rock
He casts his scattered strip,
Braces his body, tender to the shock,
And lets it gradually dip
Into a liquid seal
That covers first the heel
- Colder and rising colder -
Over the thigh, above the hip
And slinking up the side
To sheathe the slowly-sinking shoulder.
    Now he is in:
No longer naked, airy-thin:
The river holds him in a second skin,
And he is water-wide,
Fluidly formless, flowing on its tide.
And now he lunges, aquabatic eel,
To writhe and wreathe and roll and reel
And wallow on the water feel;
Till, with a reaching glide,
He grasps at rock and gets a grip
And heaves his muscles from the water's lip;
Shivers, and stands to drip,
    Shaking his hair,
Naked again, and still more bare
As droplets glisten down, and peel
His water skin into the sunlit air.

Bided Time

The rule of eye for eye and tooth for tooth
Tempered the passions of my headstrong youth.
Blinded by age, baring a toothless gum,
Old enemy, I come.

Broken Down

High waters, leeching from the cliff, recede,
And reefy rock-heads, sleek in streaming weed,
          Come up for air and sky.
Down by their tepid pools, where starfish lie,
Soft crabby spiders, small crustaceous fry,
          Hard limpets, home and dry,
Sun-coloured water snails that bask and feed,
All creeping creatures of amphibious breed
Are mergers in the sea and with the land.
So must these rocks that crumbled from the Head
          And still resistant stand
               As tides go by
Take a long road of slow and stony tread,
Leaping long groynes whose rake serrates the strand,
Boulder to grinding pebble, flint to grit
          And grit to silting sand
That shores the Crumbles, shapes the Langney spit
          And makes a water's end of it

Hard Times

     The air is stiff with cold. A vice
     Clamps on the land and tightens hold
     On waters numbed in sheeted ice,
     To firm them in a deeper mould
     And lap them with the land together.
     Flesh falls away and blood flows narrow.
Under the staring fur, the muffled feather,
          Bone is bitten to the marrow.
          Winter's features, chiselled cold,
               Are set in place.
          We live in little space,
And time is frozen for the fallen sparrow.

A Fellow of Some Standing

Before you put
Your upstart foot
Upon a millipede,
Remember he
Has pedigree:
Respect that ancient breed
That scrambled free
From ancient sea
To nibble ancient weed.
Mild herbivore,
He asks no more
Than may fulfil his need.
Along the edge
Of softish veg
He finds his frugal feed;
And once replete
He shifts his feet.
The front ones take the lead.
He never looks
At any books,
Though worms have learned to read,
Nor bends his knees
- A lot of these -
To tell a passing bead.
This little lowly
    Roly Poly
    Holds to a simple creed,
And sees his god
As Arthropod,
Segmented, multi kneed,
Most wise and just
In foot and crust
And heart and mind and deed.
O, Bipeds who
Have just come through,
All thrusting strength and speed,

Whose flailing arm
Does mostly harm,
Who stride in lust and greed,
Admire the ways
Of one whose days
Are very long indeed.

The Gravy Train

Some people take the gravy train
By coming up to snatch,
While others mournfully complain
They have no train to catch;
And many doing as they're bidden,
Hurry to get their cycles ridden,
And large statistics, neatly hidden,
Trudge their domestic patch.
Well, if you can't afford a car,
You're surely safer where you are.
We urge you to refrain
From making any peevish fuss.
We know you feel you've missed the bus,
But kindly do not bother us
Who take the gravy train.

Creator

    Upon my soul,
There must be something greater than the whole,
There must be something better than the best,
Worse than the worst,
More other than the rest.
There must be something further than the first.

Island Shore

Slow waves, discarded by the shrugging sea,
    Draw up their own identity
And lift it to a curving crest before
They trace their spreading smile across the sand
And sink beneath the never-ending shore
That runs, by cape and inlet, round the land
    And back again, for more
Slow shruggings from the sea's unending store.

Red Flower

    The poppy, stemming from the chalk,
Keeping its head well down, seems not to heed
The sudden surging of its slender stalk
    Till, at a signal earlier agreed,
        It rears a buoyant head,
Cramming the calyx, bursting from its caulk.
    Then there is freed
A crumpled flag, unfurling on the wind, and spread
    In broad, triumphant red.
    Never suppose it dead
When the last flaming fragment's shed:
Stiff-necked and wiry-stemmed, full of the seed
    Of revolutionary deed.

Dust

    Golden dust, lit pale,
    Fills the sun shaft,
Hazing with motes that weave and waft
    And fall and lift,
    And fail, and downward drift.
Let sleeping dust lie, where it spreads its veil.

Not for the World

- My oyster then, and promisingly pearled -
    Would I go back to being seventeen,
Supple, to take the strain,
The passing joy, the persevering pain
    Of all that lies between;
To learn my life by heart
    Yet never glean
What in the world our duly-acted part
    Is meant to mean.
Never, no, not for all the world, again.

Martha

Pressed to lie lonely on a couch and muse,
    The active body may refuse,
Although in no way meaning to be rude
    Or spurning solitude.
Some people find that heart and head work best
    When hands are not at rest;
And often if they seek repose it seems
The day's eyes swiftly close and shutter down the mind;
    Taut reels unwind,
Thin threads of thought rush through a falling blind
    Into a whirlpool race of spinning dreams.

Much Obliged

He had a strong feeling of Ought,
And gave obligations much thought,
And if they amounted to Must
That bound you to do it or bust:
It wasn't a thing you discussed.

Coming of Age

I fear a shrivelling, and not alone
    The sag of skin on bone,
But the slow dystrophy of muscled mind,
Hardening prejudice, with insight blind,
    Conception cut and dried;
A stoppage of compassion, pity grown
    A parasite inside
And gall compacted to a wizened stone.

Remorse of the Henchmen

They went and hit him hard across the face
Just as it took them, every little while.
It wasn't that he actually sneered -
        He couldn't smile:
    His mouth was not the place.
It was his look of seeing something vile,
    Glaring at our disgrace,
Seeing us, not as something to be feared,
        But to despise.
And then the staring bastard goes and dies,
So now that look will never leave his eyes -
His judging eyes, that looked into our case
And with supreme contempt have closed the file

Escape Dream

We seek some little hatch
    For our escape,
And find at last a door -
    It changes shape.
We never find the latch:
    That's just the catch.

The Circle

That circle may be vicious: do not try
Stroking its back - you might just poke its eye,
Since there's no telling where its head may lie.
I never liked it much - it just comes round.
Probably lonely, hasn't many friends:
Self-centred, and pursuing its own ends.
It doesn't bother me. The only sound
Or comment that it ever makes is, O!
Some people think it perfect, but I know
Better; for whether turning heads of kings
Or simply making rings
Round common people, circle's always sly
And devious, not straightforward. That is why
I've never found out what it's like inside,
In case it got on edge, and took me for a ride.

Bottled Up

Hot tears of childish rage and guilt
Once watered down what milk I spilt,
But now these pricking eyelids hold
    Sharp splinters, glassy cold.

I Keep Them Fast

I hold them in my head,
I keep them fast,
All my belovèd dead.
I who am last
And near the end of thread,
The end of tether,
I hold them in my head,
Keep them together.

Conversation

Clock I've wondered - standing here - perhaps your face
Might look a little better in a case,
Or round behind your hands, like mine?
Or could you stand it in some other place?

Me This face is not my own design -
The maker simply stamps them with our name.
There's millions on his mass production line
Though none, they say, is quite the same.

Clock That's something! Well, they're much alike to me.
I'm used to yours, and now it's past its prime,
With little pouches under nine and three,
I must concede, it bears some marks of Time.

Lot's Wife

It may have been, Lot's wife was not
Particularly fond of Lot.
They may have led the kind of life
That drew her to another wife.
If she in love was looking back
Along the disappearing track,
I shall not count it as a fault,
But say that she was worth her salt.

Father to Son

We used to stride along, while you, hard put
To match my stride, admired my extra inches,
And now the boot is on the other foot
    It pinches.

Questionnaire

(A coffee morning is taking place)

How do you like your coffee, black or white?
    Either, for me, is right.
How do you like your coffee, white or black?
    This is a little pack
Selling at Oxfam, for the benefit
Of those who plant and harvest it,
    Their working bodies nicely done
To coffee colour by a roasting sun.
How do you like your people, brown or pink
    Or yellow? Are you quite
Convinced you never made a racial slight?
    Or are you one to think
        Chinese are chink?
Do you see yellow peril from Japan?
Do you approve an immigration ban?
Should colours mix, or nations keep in place?
Are you disturbed when black and white embrace?
You fear the weaving in of coloured thread?
I see your glass is empty. White or red?
I like the red, with colour from the skin,
But grapes are very much the same within,
And that's the beauty of it: skin's not deep.
Are you still drinking at the colour bar?
Does colour count, or is it what you are
That matters? Many wines are good to keep.

And now our coffee morning will discuss
    'Who shall be one of us?'

Grot

Today I saw a plastic daff
Enduring in a concrete caff,
All grotty on a window sill,
Too dead for even looks to kill;
While on the ground below it grew
The spoil consumers cannot chew,
The plastic wraps which will not rot,
All grotty on that damnèd spot.

Esprit Fort

I am my proper counsellor,
I take my own advice,
And never toss a penny,
Never need to throw the dice.
We all have something deep inside
Which aims to be our trusty guide,
In praising virtue, blaming vice
Dependably the same.
It fills us with a proper pride
Or with a sense of shame.
So if one day I'm feeling good
I take the credit, as I should,
And if I'm feeling wicked
There is only me to blame.

Jargon

In terms of this moment in time
Our language succinctly sublime,
Is hopelessly far gone
In meaningless jargon
And covered in gormless grime.

The Eccentric

Yes, that was him, they said, all right,
Roaming about the cliffs at night,
Only the moon, no proper light,
Always a little short of sight;
Most people thought he wasn't quite . . .
Most likely uninsured, no cover,
Yes, that was him, they said, all over.

Hospital Life

Having little left to give,
Old folks lose the will to live;
Nature waits to cut the cord.
Over in the natal ward
Where a life has come awake
Hungry children learn to take.

The Mathemagicians

Look beyond
The widening circles on the sullen pond
Where the stone sank,
And follow as they spill
Into the sudden bank
And spread below the meadow, under rooted elm,
Beneath the village, through the churchyard graves
Towards the caverns underneath the farthest hill.
Here, as the mind's eye reels in a remoter realm,
Deep in the dripping dark of water caves,
Insomnient wizards numerate the waves
That wash from surfaces of land or sea
And filter them to far infinity.

Hoar Frost

On winter's wood, by dark,
Through breath of dank decay,
An icy moonshine fell
That took the breath away
And held it frozen stark
    In silent spell.
Then all the woodland, in a trice,
Was cast in crystal, etched in ice
    Under the white moon mark.

By day the moon fell dim,
But when its globe was gone
    A hoary magic shone,
    Flashing in icy fires
    From light beyond.
A crusted pool lay under starry skim,
The stricken seeded heads stood white as wand,
Slivers of moonshine glazed along the wires
    As still the frozen moon hung on
        In every rinded rim
            Of winter's limb.

Moonstrike

At the night-owl's foggy horn,
Haunting hollow, half forlorn,
Fluttered moth and skittering mice,
Sparrows twigging on the thorn,
Slinking shrews below the corn
Turn to water, turn to ice.
Soon the curving claw and beak
Strike across a moonlit streak.

The Hare

He pricks a wary ear aloft;
From birth his timid eye is peeled.
A tawny coat, all silken-soft,
Is made for merging with the field.
A hare lives on the outer edge:
No lair, no den, no bolt or burrow.
Youngsters nestle by the hedge
Or lope alertly in a furrow,
Keeping alive by taking heed,
By taking care, by taking cover
Or vanishing at lightening speed -
- Except when Spring excites the lover.

The moon of March makes all things quick,
And coupling's coming into fashion.
Now is the Hare a lunatic
Afire with procreative passion.
Nothing can scare a mad March Hare
Who now astounds with leaps and bounds,
Devil-may-care and going spare
With antics fit to fright the hounds.
Every season he begets,
But March abets one glorious fling;
So all his little leverets
Are looking forward to the Spring.

Sorrow, Sorrow

Sorrow, sorrow looms tomorrow,
Apprehension haunts today:
Soon my love must break away.
Little time is ours to borrow,
Borrow, borrow, soon to pay.

Coal

Folded below, far under folded hills,
    Old ferny forests hide
        In sunken grief
    Their fallen summer pride,
    Their shroud of shrunken leaf.
They suffer seamy change beneath the weight,
The load, of long-accumulated ills,
With all that, living, struggled, suffered, cried,
    And found in death relief.
We dig a pit through sorrows stratified,
And haul a creature past them to a brief
Living incineration. What had died,
Was buried, rose again, we shall cremate,
    And when its body chills,
Shall cast the cindered phoenix carelessly aside.

Lord of the Plane Trees

London: the sun-god, shining on the park,
    Is out to make his mark
Upon his worshippers, prostrated acolytes,
Who seek his golden touch, and at his high command,
    Careless of searing aftermath,
Scatter their brightest garments in his path.
Beware! This god is dangerous. He bites
    Even the bark
Of seasoned planes, who know just where they stand,
Out in all weathers, summer-stripped and stark.
He strokes their skin with gold, and makes them bear his brand.

End of the Climb

We climbed the peak by proxy, on the map,
Exhausted, sitting with our back
Against the wind, our back against the wall.
The contours came too close: I need more gap.
There'll come a time
I'll never climb
At all.
And so he left us, while we kept his pack.
We watched him striding upwards, bending tall,
- A wiry, nervous, energetic chap -
Saw him, much later, high and very small
Against the sky, thin-posted on the crest,
Waving in our direction, like the host
Of all the mountain, welcoming a guest.
My waving may have signalled: Be my ghost.

The Rock

The father set me thinking of a shellfish:
Hard on the crust and winkle-tough inside.
He lived there by the sea with a sad anemone,
A sea wind-flower with fronds blown open wide.
They had a daughter, solid and unselfish,
A rock eroded by the running tide.

The sea came in and out across the shingle.
It took the sad anemone one day.
She drifted out to sea, a captive broken free;
The shellfish lingered, now a limpet grey,
And cleaving to his rock with purpose single,
Hung on. The rock it was that fell away.

Geese in the Garden

Far across a sea of grass,
Trumpeting from beaks of brass,
Goose and goose and gander-mate
Spot a stranger at the gate.
On they come like ships of state,
Rocking down a grassy strait,
Broad of bows and deep of keel,
Anchored to their moving meal.
Pass politely, for they hate
Foreign footsteps on their plate,
Though they never think it rude
To put their own feet on their food.

If you ask them where they wander,
Button-eyed they pause and ponder,
But they never ruminate:
As their hold fills up with freight
All that gallonage of grass,
Processed at a constant rate,
Soon emerges, lower class,
Fresh delivered while you wait,
Freely over man's estate:
What they eat and what they ate
Come together, up to date.
Nothing will last for long - tout passe!
We shall not speak to mourn our fate
When we are pushing up the grass
For goose and goose and gander-mate.

Sounds Gone by

As sounds went singing down the road
When summer's air was pure and free
A decorous procession flowed.
It was a sight to see!
Far-reaching rustles overrode
The bird notes trickling from the hedge,
While little packs of clucks and quacks
Cavorted near the edge.
All down the crown came clomps and moos
And driven flock of rippled bleat,
With barking by the prick of feet
And cries in motley crews.
Then clip and clop with crack and creak
And flick and flop with croak and caw.
They all went down the working week
With whisperings of straw
And twilit twitch of owlet ear
And beetle tick and mouse's breath:
Those hidden sounds the earth could hear
When dark was still as death

Poor Fish

Don't cry, stinking fish,
Lying abandoned on your plate, forgotten.
We're sorry now, and wish
We hadn't left you, made you feel so rotten.
You would have been delic . . .
Oh, hush! Don't cry so loudly, stinking fish!

Making Love

He adds his sweetness to the pale, soft yeast
Of unaroused desire, soon felt;
Warms it with firm caress, and feels it melt,
And so begins their feast.
The living, loving source, released,
Slow surges through the yielded flesh, to spread
Deep in the body's vault, helpless as water shed
In struggling streams, that fill, but never slake
The thirst of cavernous hills. - Do they so ache?
And is it ecstasy, the quench of parching thirst,
As crater splits, and fiery liquids burst
From darkness, spreading in a molten lake?

Damoclesian Dance

I have been living all my life,
Like better men before me,
Below the edge of cutting knife
Discreetly poised to score me;
And had no fears
In early years
That such a fate could bore me.

I have been dancing all my life
As something pulled the string.
In footing it to flute and fife
I must have lost my spring:
In square and set
And minuet
And roses in a ring.
I have been dying all my life,
And death's the coming thing.

To a Sister

We two have stood so often, swollen-eyed
    Watching the dead descend,
    Seeing a coffin glide
With parent, husband, brother, sister, friend.
Now of our loved ones only we are left:
The next bereaved will be the most bereft.
These ancient rituals bring us no relief:
There is no way to burn or bury grief.
    Let you not come to mine,
    Let me not come to yours.
    So, keeping even scores,
    You, sitting warm indoors,
        Drink me your wine!
Or, if the elder should be taken first,
I shall not then remember you as hearsed
    And driven into flame,
    But keep you still the same,
And think of you - as you may think of me -
When, in our childhood immortality,
We swam all summer in a shining sea;
Explored the Downs as youngsters free to roam,
And took those early-morning mushrooms home
    Which you could always spot,
Having a nose for them, as I had not;
Or cycled in the country, two abreast,
To oak woods where the primroses were best,
    And picked a lovely lot.
They say the old are far too apt to yearn
For dimly-distant days of no return,
Yet our remembered lives are not more past
    Than we must be, at last.

Easy Going

I'll go along with age. I get its drift:
No longer lithe and strong, no longer swift,
Make time, and take it off.
Since there can never now be time enough
For all we planned to do, let projects fall.
Take seats in dappled sun beside the wall
And wake, surprised at being out of bed;
Read novels - (some we have already read;)
Meet friends, and colleagues oddly changed with time
Make changing rhythms rhyme;
Enjoy the guilt of sloth, forbidden fruit;
Care nothing for repute;
Approach the final, all-abiding sleep
Gently. There's no great hurry: it will keep.

Success Story

        Fortune rarely smiled
And only with her lips. She never loved
        - Not with her eyes -
The stolid, uncomplaining child
Just growing up to manly size.
The iron of her hand
Was never veiled or velvet gloved
Nor was her sudden retribution mild:
        She simply shoved
Him back and down until he almost fell
        - A boy unmanned.
Then anger steeled his arm: he broke her spell,
        Seeing how it behoved
A victim to strike out. Blindly he struck.
Now he is older, harder, and has better luck.

Setting our Sights

A sow's ear never made a silken purse.
Go for a pigskin one - you could do worse.

The Ripple 1992

It hardly made a ripple
Down here in Senna Street.
These probes behind the universe
Make nothing better, nothing worse,
Nor cut the price of tipple
Nor help to make ends meet.

What should we know of Ripple?
It's all so long ago,
And Senna Street is just a dump,
We slide downhill from slump to slump,
And unemployment's triple
And set to grow and grow.

What made the Ripple ripple?
No human brain can tell,
But works away for all it's worth,
Out to destroy our ravaged earth
And terminally cripple,
Making a human hell.

Some Done

We have left undone those,
And we have done
The other things we chose,
Which were more fun.
That is the way it goes.

Remorse

De mortuis, we say, and that's the score
For poor old Effie, who was such a bore,
So wearing, one of those
Dependent, clinging creatures, never from your door
But then she goes,
And in a while you find you miss her more
Than anyone could then suppose.
You wish she could have known, or hope she knows.

End

I will not go down cold into the dark,
But leap in searing flame
To wisp away in smoke - no mark,
Nothing, without a name.

For the Time Being

Dear Descartes,
Please tell me, where does all your thinking start?
I am because I think I am, you say.
OK
But wait -
What if the great I AM, the only great,
Who I think thinks I am,
Indulging in some temporary dream,
A sabbath sleep, not minded to create,
Has cast us simply as a passing sham,
So that we are not what we think we seem?
It seems to me,
And you, I think, might well agree,
That is no way to be.

Intimacy

Yes, we were intimate, and when we met
    The light had sudden grace.
We walked alone. No others from our set
    Intruded on our space.
Our intimacy was complete, and yet
    It never must take place.

Sad Shadow

I stood there on the hill
    In summer heat
And kept my shadow cool:
    An hour to kill.
The evening air was sweet,
For soon we two should meet
    As lovers will.
        Poor fool!
The hour went by. As if it knew,
My heart sank down; but still
The saddened shadow grew, and grew
    Thinner, more ill
        Until
Hanging on heavy feet,
    As shadows will,
It sloped off down the hill.

Trying

We are getting the knack of it,
We are over the ridge,
We have broken the back of it.
- Pity it was a bridge.

Colour Sense

I am completely blind, and I see red
    As blood, run sticky, warm,
    - The day my finger bled;
    Or, (not at all the same)
        As flame,
    As fiery storm.
Colour: I feel it in my fingertips,
    Taste with my lips.
My skin soaks up the yellow of the sun.
    Yellow. Yellow is one
Of those consoling colours, gentle heat,
    Soft, cowslip-scented, sweet.
Blue is a flower hanging like a bell;
    Is cold, no smell,
        Is dry,
The colour of a cloudless summer sky
    Above the reach of touch.
    I cannot feel it much.
Black is all mine to keep: the lack of light;
        Not white.
Bare feet brush through the grass, carpet of green.
    They say it comes between
The blue and yellow, and is calm, serene.
    So many subtle hues,
    So varied, easy to confuse!
I cannot hope to see them otherwise
    Than in the mind's inquiring eyes
        Deep hidden in my head.
            That rainbow arc
            Beyond my dark
            Does tantalise.
I am quite blind, and sometimes I see red.

(Anyone blind from birth might find this nonsense, but I have tried to imagine the situation.)

Housebound

Out of my attic window I can reach
- Beyond the rakish roofs of County Town -
A sliver of the circle of the sea,
And every day I travel to the beach.
The tide goes in and out at my command,
My feet are firm, pale salted on their brown.
They feel the pricking shingle by the sand,
They ache about the ankles as I stand
Waiting for waves to wash above the knee.
I swim far out, they soar along the land.
Say nothing to my neighbours: they're inclined
To think old people wander in their mind.

Fifty Years On

'Remember us, remember us,' they cry,
Who did not ask to fight, nor think to die.
Young lives engulfed in battle's crimson tide,
Their dreams of future happiness denied.
In alien soil their broken bodies sleep:
Their lifeless eyes now have no tears to weep
For the new order we have failed to build,
Nor sight to see their vision unfulfilled.
The silent dead through gaping wounds yet speak
Phantom words on far-blown winds that reek
Of battle-smoke and naked death and fear.
We shall betray the dead unless we hear
These cries from every far-flung soldier's grave
For right and freedom that they died to save.

1995

Getting Ready

Nobody asked if I wanted to be.
There may have been asking, it wasn't of me
Which is why, as we die, I feel perfectly free
To pack up and go when I'm ready.

Consulted old Conscience, who didn't forbid it,
Just said be considerate, mind how I did it.
I made preparation and carefully hid it
To pack up and go when I'm ready.

Firelight

She closed the curtains, kept the firelight in.
And waiting shadows trembled on the wall,
    Spindly and flicker thin;
But when he leapt the stairs and strode the hall
And slammed the door behind and cried her name
The shadows jumped for joy in sudden flame.

Guilty Going

The bags are packed, the labels show
We're all geared up and set to go
But I'm feeling a little bit flat.
When we get home in a month or less
The garden will be in a fearful mess
But I think I can bear with that.
A kindly neighbour will cope tomorrow,
But Oh, today, reproachful sorrow!
Puddy is smelling a rat.
How do these queer little creatures tell?
I like a rest and a change, but hell!
I do hate leaving the cat!

Her Face

She smiled at me. Her face, so fair and frail,
Has hung its bramble blossom wild
Across my waking eyes, and if I sleep, the pale
Fine petals, faintly pink, that smiled,
Dance in my dark lids, joyfully beguiled,
Tangle my dreams in a long bramble trail.

Introspection

I don't suppose you often do, but if
We sit and contemplate our umbilicus
One merry thought is almost bound to strike us:
How many more are manufactured like us,
Knotted like packages around midriff,
  Cut from the cord,
    Fresh made,
Upon an endless moving belt conveyed,
One by the other, all across the board.
  What's yours is much the same as mine
    On our production line.
For those who would be masters of their fate
The navel's not a thing to contemplate.

Forsaken

Cold as a stone, the cockles of my heart
Lie heavy, fallen. If we are to part,
That warmth, which melted all my breast and flowed
In breathless coursing, till the arms would ache,
Cannot, with dropping of a stone, forsake,
But burns within the cold. So stones explode.

In the Wilderness

No lawful fixed abode,
Only a goatskin stretched below the stars,
A hearth that gathers by the water jars,
A few belongings stowed.
The nomads move along by law of need
To reach a rock where living water flows,
To camp a while where meagre pasture grows
And scraggy goats may feed.
They trek their life along a dusty road,
Whipped by the wind, with hunger for their goad,
Fettered by tethers, held by hidden bars.

Their narrow world moves on; and camp fires burn
The dark; day rises into heat and dust.
Jehovah may be merciful, though stern,
And as they deem him just
There blossoms in the desert growing trust
Of One who says, You shall not, and, You must,
And makes the crusted constellations turn.

Going Carefully

Bearing these years, I'm careful how I go.
I watch my step, and sigh to see it slow.
Is that the time?
How soon it races by! - At such a rate
The old are often vague about the date.
We stumble on, downhill: it seems a climb.
Now rush hours jostle past, as if to brush
The elderly aside. Perhaps they wait
And gather round behind - to give a push.

He Took His Own

Now that his life is sad and gone
That had endured too long,
I shall not sing for such a one
      A mourning song.

He gave as much as all who give
The little that they have,
Took only what was his to live,
      Greeted the grave.

The mound is low, the world is wide,
In time he'll be forgot:
Not resting, not in hope abiding,
      Not.

Panic Pipe

I made to whistle in the dark
As I walked over Capers Hill,
Alone, when every hush was still:
No call, no distant bark.

The Down shone pale, the moon was bare.
A whistle keeps us free from care.
A man may whistle if he will:
It well becomes a man.

My breath came out so piping shrill
I took my heels and ran.
Ah, whistle if you can,
Tearing like wind down Capers Hill
Pursued by jealous Pan.

The Quest

In the pursuit of happiness
I never galloped in a coat of red
Nor put on any style of hunting dress.
I used to stalk it through the summer trees,
Scenting its flutter on the laden breeze.
Some captured it. I was not one of these,
But sought to glimpse it in the path ahead,
    Sighting it as it fled.
I never took a gun to shoot it dead,
    Nor any gin, nor net,
    But if we ever met
I hoped, by use of certain spells and charms,
    To catch it in my arms
And hold it captive in that cunning snare.
But I have never really seen it yet,
    And if I ever did,
Perhaps I'd have to leave it where it hid,
And it would never know that I was there.

Intensive Care

    There is no splint:
I never wore my heart upon my sleeve,
But then, it was not free to roam about.
    Now it is taken out,
And here I lie, with lint
Caught half inside the healing wound. I leave
Things very still. I do not stir, nor shout,
    And that by dint
Of feeling all my flesh become as flint.
    But the old wound will grieve.

Disillusion

Now that I know your feet are feet of clay
I've taken that old pedestal away
That bowled along, by miracle, beneath,
    Circled by rosy wreath,
And kept you lofty in a moving shrine.
So now your feet are nearly down to mine,
    Are nearly down to earth;
Yet even common clay has certain worth.
Could we still walk and talk, along the former line?
- But now I see there's nothing more to say:
Your feet are taking you another way.

Mud Styx

    They tell me I'm just
    A collection of dust,
And my bones can be burnt into ash.
    It's clearly implied
    That there's little inside
Except water, so settle my hash
    And I'll take the whole mix
    To the banks of the Styx
And immerse with a muddy old splash.

The Looker On

It called for protest. I was stricken dumb.
I called for courage, but it didn't come.
They bound their prisoner. My limbs are free,
But not the heart of me,
Which feels itself in tainted honour bound
To strike . . . or take some action . . . make some sound.

The Rabbits are Back

Humanly speaking, bunny rabbits
Have very antisocial habits,
While from a coney point of view
The same is true of me and you.
That furry felon's barely born,
He's got his nibblers in your corn,
Your peas, your carrot crop - you name it -
No matter how you fence and frame it
With sticks and wire and bits of tin,
Those beastly bunnies muscle in.
Well, finally we paid our sub
And joined the local rabbit club.
- No, not a case of beat or join 'em:
Its sole objective was destroyin' 'em.
Then that broke up for lack of money
And notched another up to bunny.
So that was when I got a gun
And sat beside a rabbit run,
And saw reproachful Lewis Caroll
Sitting astride the double barrel,
And dreamt o' nights of Beatrix Potter
Baring her teeth and snarling, Rotter!
While tiny shapes in frisky fur
Held out a paw and shouted, Brer!
I got this dreadful sense of guilt
Before much blood was ever spilt;
-And as I'm such a rotten shot
I must confess that much was not -
Spent hour,of anguish in my hide
- Till mothers brought their young inside!
So now I'm moving into town,
For Watership has got me Down.

The Chocoholic

She was not one for peppermint
Or butterscotch or rock,
She was a chocoholic and
She battened on the choc.
She battened and she fattened and
Became an awful crock;
She died, and at the autopsy
They had an awful shock:
Choc-full she was of chocolate,
Her tubes were choc-a-block.

Martello

(In praise of a favourite minor architect)

Admire the skill of Mythical Martello
Who, ever since he was a little fellow,
Had toiled upon the sand with pail and spade,
Learning the secrets of his later trade.
Here stands his martial monument, which humbles
The proud invader, dominates the Crumbles!
Moulded in symmetry, raised in the round,
On some enchanted circle in the ground,
This sturdy turret stands, so stout and true
To prototype: it must be solid through!
- Oh happy sandboy, who could tilt his pail
On such a bold, Napoleonic scale!

Playing Safe

He stood up to be counted,
Entertained a trace of doubt,
And sat there on the sidelines
While the rest were counted out.

Human

Beware! It is a human thing,
Having no poisoned bite nor sting,
Glazing no eye of basilisk,
But yet a calculated risk.
I cannot love all human kind,
And treat with caution as I find,
Mistrustful of the ways of man,
Being a member of his clan.

Night Trains

Stillness of falling night when I was young
Lifted the distant sounds of day and flung
Them nearer; and the trains went out to sea.
        - Or so it seemed to me,
Who, narrow in the bed, though wide awake,
Heeded their warning whistle on the wave,
The clank of couplings down the water-snake.
Then all the creaks and sighs old houses have
Crept to the door and funnelled through the lock,
While every quarter hour the Town Hall Clock
Struck nearer: it had moved another block.
We had no global circuit then for sound,
Although it travelled through the telephones,
So echoes used to like to move around
On trains that crossed the moonlit pebblestones
Into the Channel, where they nightly steamed
Along the water-line, out where the lightship gleamed.

Hopeful Quest

The vast expanding loom of time and space
That weaves its seamless pattern star by star
Affords humanity no pride of place:
They lost the thread before it took them far.

Immensity in millions scales to nought
The short gyration of their satellite;
Yet they were rational, or so they thought,
With some vestigial sense of wrong and right.

Questing like gods, with minds of mortal men,
They strove to fathom, analyse, define,
Patiently probing how and where and when
From intricacies of a great design;

And sometimes, not expecting a reply,
Pondered their strange position, wondered, why?

I had a Window

I had a window open to the sea
When summer sun lay yellow on the sand;
A place of sure retreat, a place to be,
With all the open waters to command
    There on the edge of land
Where sun and wind and wave should well agree.

Winter. The Channel horses, broken free,
Came charging down the bay with flowing mane
To paw the shore and foam the churning scree.
One lunging steed reared up, and hurled a rain
    Of pebbles at the pane.
- I had a window open to the sea.

Fishing Idyll

There is a spot along a reedy bank,
Sought on a greying Sunday afternoon,
Where fishes rise, and late a fish-hook sank.
The muddy slope behind the man is strewn
    With tackle and with baits;
    And there his fond love waits:
She who, inured to tang of tench and dace,
Prepares and serves, yet could not share the spoils,
Partners once more his staunch, unswerving chase;
Unpacks her bundle, winds her wool from coils,
    Dumbly and damply sits
        And knits.

No fish is stirring, but the silence breeds
A sere and soulful sighing in the reeds.
The church clock strikes again up on the hill,
Then, in a stricken silence, all is still.
    Oh, who would ever think
- Admiring such endurance on the brink -
That, Sunday-schooled in sabbath-resting murk,
    Grinning, the fishes lurk?
But now the sullen water shivers, frowns,
    A water boatmen nearly drowns.
That fisherfemale, void of rod and spool,
Has butterfingered on her ball of wool,
And now she pulls upon her puny line
And broken is the stillness: This one's mine!

Remembered Days

Those were the days, those were the days,
Seen through a fair, nostalgic haze
If we could see them full and plain
Should we beseech them back again?

End of Drought

Silent birds sit feather-still.
Thunder, prowling round the hill,
Dispels the midges' dance.
Across a staring countryside
Rigid corn stands petrified,
The trees are in a trance.
A haunting spectre, boding ill,
Looming nearer, out to kill,
Fingers his flaming lance,
A brooding time, no place to hide;
Yet now the storm cloud, spreading wide
With spattering overspill,
Sends torrents of releasing rain.
The valley rouses, breathes again,
The rain butts sweetly fill.

Grub in Spring

How mercifully short is Feb.
When life is at its lowest ebb
And birds are living on their fat
With none too much of that.
Then, as the year moves into March
Kind nature makes a little starch,
And when the lowly proteins peep
Their life is holden cheap.
That is the very nub of spring
And possibly the only thing
That makes the early throstle sing
In rapturous refrain.
If life can fairly be construed
As hunger in pursuit of food,
The throstle sings because its brood
Is born well up the chain.

Late Spring

Winter went into March, and snow still lay
In huddles under hedges, candle-gutter grey.
Spring was still gallivanting, on a cruise
Round the Greek islands, loth to travel north.
And when she came - by air, no time to lose -
Crocus came out to greet her, bursting forth
To hold her sunlight in a golden cup;
While winter slept, worn out with waiting up.

Swans Coming Down

Angels are bending low. Their flight is fanned,
And harmony strikes in their wings. They make
    A bird line for the lake,
Sweeping with clouds of glory down, to land
    With gliding skim
On water; walk upon it; understand
Mortality, settle to sink or swim.

Night Walk Over the Seven Sisters

The moon has risen, full and bare, to ride
Above the hilltop where the cliffs begin
Their seven-fold divide
And front the smuggled waters creeping in.
The moon is ours, to guide
Descending shadows' giant-scissored stride,
Our crouching stumble up another side,
Our silent standing, thin,
Above a vast horizon curving wide,
The sky beset with starry underspin
And waters where the moon has cast aside
    A silver-scaly skin
To float the surface of a flowing tide.

Long Wind

Long and bitter blows a wind
      Under shriven sky.
Scattered cliff-top flints are skinned,
Ploughland clods sit sharp and dry.
The wind has whet its keenest blade
To hone the hillside, shear the huddled tree;
And all the open fields are flayed,
The marshes swept towards the sea.
It carves the dunes, the land's last shifting ledge
Where gaping grasses and the sea-bent sedge,
Torn shoreward, grasping at the land,
Hang on and hold it pinned
With grappled foot and wiry knotted hand,
Giving the wind its utmost edge.

Sheffield Park

Mostly they come in pairs, more old than young;
No hurry, often with a stick or stoop;
      Some with a joyful group
Of children and their children: three degrees
Who wander, staid or playful, as they please,
      A camera shoulder-slung.
Mostly they come to marvel, come to gaze
On bounteous blossom by the winding ways
Whose secret shrubs the children hide among.
      They saunter at their ease
Beside a lake, where deep reflections, hung
Below the soaring height of mirrored trees,
Lie steeped in calm beneath the water's glaze.
Nature is stately here. Great trees have sprung,
Structured by centuries of lordly days;
And autumn's glory sets them all ablaze,
Richly resplendent, rather old than young.

Dung Beetle

Behold a lowly beetle from the very bottom rung,
Just eating and excreting and begetting of my young.
I am mild and pleasant-mannered, and I never bit or stung,
I'm utterly dependable, not wild or highly-strung.
They tell me there's a universe exceedingly far flung,
But Chafer feels much safer when he's sitting on the dung,
Though not the sort of sitter who would get his portrait hung.
I was not made for singing, so my song will not be sung;
I fall upon my back and die, your withers are unwrung;
Yet still I'm clinging to the hope to which I've always clung:
That I may meet my Maker, the eternal heaps among.

Horse and Groom

Down at the inn they meet to drink.
(No parching tongues, no bursting throats.)
So many dapper coats of pink,
　　So many black
　　And dapper coats!
So glossy every horse's back,
　　So silken sleek the pack!
Says Ferdie Fox, It's odd to think
So many dapper coats should rush
Like mad to catch one little brush.

Release

The very time is ripe! Our orchards stand
Agog with apples looking for a hand
To cup them to the pail,
Or swirling autumn gale
To hurl them headlong on the grassy land.
Release is in the air, their link grows frail,
And as the last comes leaping down, a tree
　　May shake its branches free.

Growth

When first I guileless to a garden came
It seemed a blessed haven of repose;
Once down to earth, with spades and hacking hoes,
I had no policy to kill or maim.

But found I had to do it all the same.
Stark stands the choice: the greenfly or the rose?
The dolphin or the slug? And so I chose
To kill, to cure, to bear the Buddha's blame.

Connived infliction, met conflicting claim.
You never spread your fingers, tread your toes,
But some small underling that undergoes
Is quietly screaming, crushed or fallen lame.

Death and decay: by such my garden grows.
Our growing is a gruesome thing, God knows!

Lone Creature

I never knew a chestnut from a bay,
And how to speak to horses - no idea;
And yet it came about, I had to stay
And mutter something in its twitching ear
And reach to give its neck a kind of pat.
The very field was lorn. A mist hung drear
From hedge to hedge, the grass grew out of grey,
    And not a soul was near.
When I could think of nothing more to say
        I came away
    And brought myself back here.
I paced a while about the silent flat,
        And that was that.

The Hearth

So here I sit
- Now quick to tire -
Stare at a fire
Another lit.

Cinders I swept
Each winter day,
Took out the grey,
The black I kept.

He sawed the wood,
He stacked it by,
And he and I
Were warm and good.

In winter storm
Our flame leapt high,
And he and I
Were good and warm.

I would as soon
The hearth were dead
As see it red
And sit alone.

High Summer

Now summer spreads a leafy sky
And half the hedge is hidden high
    In points of parsley lace.
The air goes up and up and into space,
And leafy- shadowed sun falls where you lie
And dapples light upon your upturned face.

A Pox on it

It's something of a paradox
That putting four wheels round a box
And setting light to things inside
Should take a country for a ride.
The ancient village steeple rocks
Before the juddernaut, and - worse -
Cripples and corpses, nervous crocks,
Arouse but transient remorse.
Run over? No, they just collide.
Sad families are wrenched by force
From homes demolished in the course
Of sinking half the countryside
In concrete under traffic blocks.
See how I mount my hobby horse
(Although I drive a car, of course,)
And , firm astride, pronounce a pox,
A murrain, on the motor box.

Screwmatics

Old Mr Ades was bent
Almost in two. His grey head went
Along beside the infant's - but the boy looked up.
Not much he hadn't done of things that meant
Others' survival: singled, reaped and mown,
Helped milking, calving, cared for teg and tup,
Laid hedges, stacked and thatched, borne on his own
Great sacks that went at sixteen stone.
And now the 'screws' has got him: almost turned
Full circle. That was what he earned.

The Purpose

    A woman trudged her life,
Shopping around a penny-pinch bazaar
Where shoddy, brittle objects, made to mar
In multiple, were all that lay in store:
Little of worth, yet pilfering was rife.
A thief might bear his booty to the door,
But greed and cunning could not get him far:
There was no street outside. Others checked out and paid
            When they could bear no more,
But in the doorway stopped and made
            To come back in, afraid.
    The woman saw, up on a shelf
Where one by reaching high could help himself,
    Offered, a precious jar,
Flawless, in shape and lustre, without par.
But, said the woman, trudging, What's it For?

Hard Horizon

Mine is a ship set in a circled sea
That curves the sloping sky on every hand.
Drawn by the limits of the human eye,
Unending waters meet unending sky,
Excluding from us their infinity
With an unfathomable, endless band.
Here I can see no land,
No rock with rooted tree,
Only that hard, encompassing embrace
Holding great waters, with their changing face.

Here I Sit

Now only, in the winter of my time,
Close to the snow peak of an arduous climb,
Let me sit by, look down to greener slopes,
Through grief and fears and joyful springing hopes

To those I loved, who left me far behind,
But reappear, by vision of the mind,
Just where they were, and looked, with what they said;
Though distant, still distinct, alive, though dead.

When life is long the final climb is steep.
A frail old body fears the final leap,
When, scant of energy and short of breath,
The old heart fails, its body tired to death.

Some clamber on, some stand and wait for it;
I have gone far enough, and here I sit.

Long Bond

Time out of mind
- Some powers of memory are fledged and flown -
We two have lived in harmony together,
Thinking each other's thoughts, till we are grown
Birds of a feather;
Not owls or eagles, not so wise, more blind.
When all is said and done in years behind,
We like to be together on our own
In friendly silences. Yet each, we find,
If left alone,
Talks to ourself, in a low undertone.

The Upright Man

He had an old Upright
- A bike, not piano -
For keeping mens sana
In corpore sano.
Its handlebars lofty,
Unchanging its gear,
He pedalled it forte
And played it by ear.

He had an old Brownie
- A camera, not kobold -
That always went with him
Wherever he wobbold.
And if he saw something
He cared to take home,
He soon snapped it up
In a pale monochrome.

He had an old Bowler
- Now that isn't cricket -
Which sometimes blew off:
There was no way to stick it.
I don't think he wore it
Because it was shady:
He just liked to lift it
When passing a lady.

As Nice an old Fellow
- Precise but not Prof -
As ever kept Upright
And carried it off.

On Women

This variant of Homo Sap
Is best considered as a lap:
An ample soft amorphous thing
Surmounted by an apron string
To which the male, as soon as hatched,
Remains despondently attached.
Its gleams of light are far and few.
It never thinks, but Always Knew,
Viewing all nature with distrust
It chases particles of dust;
Abhors invention, cleaves to habit
And reproduces like the rabbit;
Allows its mate to work and sleep,
Refuses him the right to weep;
Delights to be considered frail
Yet normally survives the male;
However, as their lives are linked,
Will soon (V Rabbit) be extinct.

The Fright

He came too late: lo, there she lay:
Her lips already cold and grey
Within a ghastly mask of clay.
Oh, hapless fate!
Look well, O man, this is the face
That shall your dinner table grace
Tonight at eight.
You came too early, not too late.

The Tower of Babel

Now man is getting up to tricks,
Neglecting stone and making bricks,
And learning in the course of time
That if you take a lump of lime
And water down to make a slime,
It sticks.
Presented on another plane:
Man grows ingenious, but vain.
Now, folks in towns are ill-advised
To count themselves more civilised;
In fact, the higher they are rised
The more they fall from glory.
So do not live in ziggurats
Or up in blocks of penthouse flats
In case you get cut off - and that's
The moral of my story.

Communication is a word
No little Shemite ever heard
Before the Great Divide occurred
They simply met to chatter.
But once they built a tower so high
It posed a threat against the sky.
They should have built it flatter.
For naturally God was vexed
To see a poking finger flexed
So high in his direction.
He shook their ladders, broke the rungs
And set them learning foreign tongues:
Their whole was cut in section.
They shouted fit to burst their lungs,
As people do, in foreign tongues
When talking to a native;
And some of them were horrified
To find they had to use a guide
To get down to the dative;

While others had to read the blurb
To find out where to put the verb:
A situation to disturb
Even the most loquacious.
It was the start of Thomas Cook's,
Of Europe's dreary grammar books
And even more of Asia's.

Rise up in heart and mind and steeple
But do not build too high, good people.

Thirties Fair

When Johnny was a long time at the fair
His forehead lost its usual cautious frown.
He tossed away dull care
Of daily service, earning half a crown.
He spent a little more than he could spare
On boating in the swings,
And rose up high and higher in the air
Simply by pulling strings;
Snared a cheap vase with one of twenty rings
And took a pot shot in a rifle booth,
Had an old gypsy say him sooth,
And paid to see a freak, but could not stare.
Then, bashful, on the ghost train made a pair.
(No fun unless you raise a maiden's hair!)
And drank a pint of bitter down.
So in the end he hadn't got his fare:
A long walk home. He ran his money out
Setting off gaily on the roundabout
That was why Johnny was a long time there.

The Last Minute

As earth's old heart is ticking to a close
The pulse of self, on evolution's thrust,
Throbs madly in an all consuming lust
To kill, destroy; to shape, control, dispose
Like God Almighty, powerful and freed
From all constraint, while every wind that blows
Raises a barren dust.
Are we insatiable, so full of greed
We cannot spare the crust
Of earth, nor share with neighbours in their need?
There comes a time we must.
Late in the day, we falter, hesitate,
Watching the balance of our measured time,
And mark the wasting hours' relentless chime,
Their steady beat which has no heart to wait.

Friends of the Earth

I'll do no harm - No good! In being born
We make that hope forlorn.
I'll live to do some good. No harm in trying,
But more we do in dying.

No Fairy Tale

They lived quite happily after,
Though happily not too long.
They shared occasional laughter,
They sang occasional song;
But vainly longed to help reverse
A creeping chaos, growing worse
As right succumbs to wrong.

The Sound of Shape

Shed on a lighted screen
Is seen
The changing shape of sound
As blood is beat around,
As whistle pierces high.
What lighted graph
Could show, in the mind's eye,
The sweet shapes of your happy laugh?
What sorrow, so to hear
In the mind's ear
The long, slow trickle of your falling tear!

In Two Minds

I think I'll be
A Manichee
On what I've just divined,
From matter, anti-matter
Posing mind and anti-mind.
The former eats the latter
In a spiral's vicious wind,
And the latter eats the former
- Does it make us any warmer? -
And it all seems so unkind
I doubt if we've the Energy
To Matter or to Mind.

Supping with the Devil

It's a long spoon for the large bowl,
It's a long start for the flight,
It's a long poke with a barge pole
For the rascals on the right.

Negatives

Up in the attic of the mind
Beyond the furthest floor,
Where broken spiral stairways wind
To seek a secret door,
Old negatives, a life away,
Have never seen the light of day.
A spool of shadows, phantom show
In undeveloped night,
May, as the tenant has to go,
Come finally to light.

Looking Up

The ceiling under which I lie
Recumbent, broken-backed,
Seems warm and friendly, not too high.
And intricately cracked.
In such a long, constraining rest
There is a certain interest
In tracing human features,
And by the changing light of day
I turn them round another way,
Evolving curious creatures.

The matron said, 'We must afford
To decorate this slum!'
They'll move me to another ward
Before the workmen come.
And when they move me back again
To lie as I have always lain
Since meeting my disaster,
The ceiling will be stiff and white,
Without a living scene in sight.
We'll both be set in plaster.

Rebekah

Precious the living water!
Send a daughter:
She will bear
Brimming pitcher up the hill,
Up a steep and rocky stair,
Taking care
Nothing spill.
Only a drop of sweat
Shall wet
Her flowing hair.

Precious the living daughter,
Clear as water,
Giving birth,
Growing to a stranger's hearth,
Bearing in a careful jar
At the other end of earth;
Told by a northern star
How far, how far
Her parents are.

Nemesis

I had a nasty feeling Nemesis
Was lurking somewhere on the premises
When I got home that night.
It came upon me halfway up the stair.
I shut the bedroom door, put on the light
And saw your section of the wardrobe bare.
So I was right,
For there was no-one there.

Firework

Rising in golden rain against the stark
Night of the falling firmament, far flung
    In over-reaching arc
And slow cascading fall to the last hung
        Spark
Against the hanging blackness, swallowed, spent,
A life of loving made its fiery mark
    Across the spinning dark,
        And meant
A glimmer where the pall was rent.

Day of Rest

Sunday: licence to lie
    Till the sun's high.
    Hardly a car goes early by.
    And never one takes me.
This is the day we even grant the car
    Licence to do as others are,
Until it has its wash, fills up with tea,
    Petrol and family,
And takes the tide which sweeps towards the sea.

The Flail

    Sharp skirl
Of stinging summer hail
    Flicks wing and tail
As hard and mean as barley pearl;
Flattens the corn and cuts the kale.
All that grew strong and hale
    Proves summer-frail.

Night Breakers

Under a scudding moon long breakers roll,
        Taking their shingle toll
        In thunder on the beach,
Heaving it high with wrested undertow:
        A steady, slow
        And unrelenting leach.
The scouring sea's unceasing flow
        Leaves nothing whole;
Batters the rock-face, swirls into the breach.
Lucky the scudding moon sails out of reach!

Immortality

Those who believe
Hold all eternity within the sleeve
Of mortal dress;
For if they lose it when they go,
They will not know.
True children of an age
Of doubtful guess,
Can we but grieve
To be apportioned less?
Let not the heathen rage,
Bitter, or in despair,
Hang on to hope, that caught
In God's eternal thought,
We might stay there.

Prepared

I lurk in this valley of shame and of sorrow
And live on the time that we ancients must borrow
But wanting to know what will happen tomorrow
        Is keeping me still at the ready.

Day of Reckoning

It seems an age since I was taught
That two and two were four
And three and three two more
And five and five were one and nought
And that made half a score.
And now we find - who could have thought?
Computer chips galore.
I cannot love them as I ought
Nor know what they are for:
- Worse reckonings in store!

Militant Marchers

Like a flock of bleating sheep,
Flowing forward, thousands deep,
See the surge of chanting men
Led as to a branding pen,
Foreleg held up high to Allah
Or the gods of some Valhalla.
Shepherds watch this feckless flock,
Calculating, taking stock.

Wrong Premises

They scratched their eggheads, set their teeth
And searched above and underneath.
They wondered why it took so long.
What if their premises were wrong?
Their mathematics makes it worse
To comprehend a universe.
- Leave us the sun and moon, in sky
Which most believe is full of pi.

Tell Tale

He shot an arrow in the air:
It whistled through his offspring's hair,
The apple split in twain.
The lad felt quivers down his calves.
(Some folk hate doing things by halves.)
I think he felt the strain.
If some of you should feel appalled
- Particularly if you're bald -
Don't write up to complain.
Gone are the days of Tell and Hood,
And modern archery is good
For steady hand and brain.
Procedure nowadays is strict:
A target set, no apples picked,
No human hair so much as nicked.
It won't occur again.

Retirement

I have too long been duty bound,
Bound and delivered on a daily round;
Never had vision far above a mound,
A mole's own mountain, icebergs underground
Of worry: one care taken, others found.
Ticking away, old timepiece fully wound,
I rarely saw the sky - my nose was ground.
Now they are opening my pound.
Open my eyes again, my ears!
Give me a few more years -
Time to extend my vision, make a note of sound.

Water Lilies

Below a stream of softly-swaying weed,
Where water wallows with a loving greed
Or sluggish lies and slimes the oozing earth,
A lotus fruit has spawned its ripened seed,
And seed has given birth.
Dimly conceived, from root to breaking bud,
A vision struggles upward through the mud:
Some Dreamer's idle notion of the nenuphar.

Then, in the silted water-course of time,
Sidereal in unconsidered slime,
From fleshy foothold, through consenting dark,
It rears its groping arms and with sublime
Perception lifts them high
To rise where water holds the mirrored sky.
And here each lays its leaf in shining arc,
Or spreads its flower full circle, as a floating star.

Before the night pricks out its points of gold,
And water lies in light from ages old
Far fallen through unconscionable hours,
The lilies close with evening, sepals fold
To shield the starry flowers
From aspiration into greater dark,
Keeping them rooted here, to make their mark,
Rafted on reedy waters, never floating far.

Some Goldsmith there may be, his mind a vast
Continuum of present and of past,
Who makes the crusted constellations turn,
Who wrought our world where nothing lives to last.
Now thrusting humans burn
To rake a moonface, to corrupt the airs.
Could we not cherish earth and all it bears,
Considering the lilies, being what we are?

A Submission

Dear Sir or Madam, source of all creation,
- (No earthly need, of course, for me to write
What is already open to your sight) -
I beg you to accept my resignation.
You see that I am filled with fear and awe:
Before I knew to fear, you saw.
You knew I fancied I was some relation,
Child to a Father of prodigious height,
Because another Son had put it right
I was legitimate, within your law.
I had ideas, it seems, above my station.
Now love is torn away; my heart is raw,
Yet ticking over in appointed fashion.
Hopes of eternity recede, withdraw
From creatures cast in clay, from men of straw;
Yet days go by, and hearts beat through the night
Even without the light.
And so I humbly tender what is yours by right,
And beg you to accept my resignation.

Death Wish

Let me not wake: the point of light is gone,
I lie alone.
Worst is the waking, when disturbing day
Stares through the window. Take the light away!
Vacant is day's uncomprehending grin.
Let there be dark, and let me breathe it in,
Sink in its depth and drown within its void
            Till light be all destroyed.

A Mouse

A mouse, still young, but steeped in sin,
Once crept inside a treacle tin,
A crime his mother had forbidden,
But someone hadn't put the lid on,
And there it lay, upon its side,
And looked a lovely place to hide.
He only meant to stay a minute
To find out what the tin had in it,
But, seeing it so nearly emptied,
The little mouse was sorely tempted
To finish off what others started.
Meanwhile his mother, broken hearted,
Was riffling through her milling brood
To find which one it must be who'd
Deserted the familial nest.
It's him, she wailed. I might have guessed!
Her errant child had got his whiskers
Well stuck in it. The stuff was viscous
And sickly sweet - the best molasses,
So very soon he'd eaten masses.
Then, fearful lest he might be sick,
He made as if to beat it quick
When someone stood the tin upright.
The little mouse's face went white
- As far as one could see beneath
The fare in which he'd set his teeth;
For now it seemed as if our friend
Was coming to a sticky end.
That is exactly where he stood,
Regretting he had not been good.
At last he thought, I can but try
To be prehensile, like a fly.
Treacle is a funny stuff to stamp on,
But makes an admirable crampon
As long as you are small and light
And have the sense to hang on tight.

This little mouse was full of pluck.
Though once he nearly came unstuck
His ploy enabled him to shin
Quite smartly up the treacle tin
And patter home, where he confessed,
And got the treacle off his chest.

No Smoke

The blazing bonfire dies.
Just poke
To see faint wizened wisps arise.
They languish on the heavy air,
Expire
Above their fallen funeral pyre
And are no longer anywhere.
Their fire is out. Without a fire -
No smoke.

Work Satisfaction

The humble bee, a worker, communist,
Is never seen to clench his fist,
Nor does he know a hammer from a sickle.
He has this routine job - to tickle
The sweetest blossoms growing in his sector,
And he has been promoted works inspector.
When he and I were once at odds
I called out to him. Hey, you!
You great big bumbling berk,
If they don't pay you,
What do you get for all your work?
He told me, Nectar,
As drunk by all the gods.

Winter's End

Once the blackthorn starts to thaw
Winter stands at end of tether.
Though the wind blows bleak and raw,
Driving daffodils together,
Soon the stilling of the shaw,
Resting feather, sitting straw
Will mark the ending of the old man's law.
Furiously he tries to cling
To office. Let him have his final fling.

Rising Sap

Now Spring in bud is bursting out,
Who shall be first to cast a clout?
Rain comes scudding on the wind,
Frost has nipped the blossom's setting,
Carrots cluster to be thinned,
Lambs are fretting,
Geese begetting,
Seaside bedrooms up for letting;
Time when every Dick and Tom is
Eliciting a maiden's promise,
And for every other Harry
Time of leaping off to marry;
Of rising sap,
Of setting cap,
Of country Hamlet's head in lap;
When, unafraid of autumn rust,
The sharp new leaves are cut and thrust;
When crumbling earth is split asunder
By so much nosing up from under.
If I should ever die in Spring,
Plant me beside some struggling thing
And tie it to my marking stick:
I'll do my best to keep it quick.

Slow Land

The rains are fallen, and the storms abate.
Waters that washed these meadows in their spate
Have slithered down the banks, and lazy lie,
Letting the land go by:
Green levels, placid pasture land, inclined
To gliding motion, where the cattle stand
Idle as water, heavy as the clay
That bears them backward on its moving band,
To tread the brink of green above the grey;
Slow-drifting flats, that bring the sea behind,
And bear tomorrow back towards today,
Till water turns to brine, and clay to sand,
And sleeping springs awaken, running out of land.

Tractor Driver

The early farmer put his hand to plough
And looked not back; but things are different now:
    The coulter carves its track
    Behind the tractor driver's back.
Tilted in body, keeping straight in mind,
He turns to watch the furrows turn behind.
And still the birds come autumn-falling down,
Gulls, fishing inland, white upon the brown,
Sharp starlings, wagtails and the wary plover
        Lured from his cover.
    And there a rabbit by the shaw
        Hears the rook's warning caw
    But never troubles to retreat,
Seeing the friendly monster has no feet.
So times and ways may change, but still a band
Of husbandmen turns out to turn the land
And earn our bread - though not, we must allow,
By ancient scriptural sweating of the brow.

Noisy Squatters

Our early birds are in the bedroom wall
Between the daub and wattle and the tile,
Dragging in heavy furniture and all,
'Living it up' in style.
Soon they'll be sitting quietly on their clutch?
Not much!
In hobnailed boots they must be playing ball.
- With eggs? Now there's a prospect to appal!
But nights go by, and in a little while
One morning we shall hear a hungry cheep.
Then a frenetic squall
Will constitute our early morning call,
Ending all feathered sleep.

Ten Acre Wood

Deep in ten acre wood
A quiet time I stood
And listened to the swelling of a sound,
A sigh of sylvan stirrings all around.
Then all fell still:
The bird song and the bumble humming bees;
No breeze,
Only the deep, deep breathing of the trees,
A breath so dread, so chill,
Boding no good,
The human, in a panic, lost her head,
Stumbling fled.

The Old Walk

Across the flinty downland chalk
From Birling Gap to Cuckmere mouth
The Seven Sisters of the south
Have spread their seven cloaks of green.
So white the cliff, the curve so clean!
It used to be our chosen walk:
A steep assignment there and back.
We sat above the river, seen
With sunlight on its coiling tack.

And still we cleave to what has been.
Taking the valley where the crow
Has found his crafty way to go,
Over no hills but in between.
Here, in their sisterly embrace,
The sea and sky before our face,
We watch the crawling waves below,
The ancient sea, determined, slow.

Under a Cloud

The mist comes down with evening, like a sigh,
Casting a vague and lingering reproof.
The hills have shrunk away, a surly sky
Leans on the roof.
The lamps hang baffled, blurred.
Nothing is clearly stated, much inferred
Through seeping darkness, shadowing and sly,
Like dim suspicion hanging round for proof.

Plain from Above

There is a hilltop where I like to stand
And look across the spread of lying land,
Piecing the pattern of the quilted fields
Whose fabric mellows with their ripening yields:
A still serenity, set far and fair
Under the awning of enchanted air.
So high upon the hilltop, we forget
    The labour of the earth,
    The thrusting pang, the sweat
That reproduces death-inducing birth.
    We gaze upon the plain
And make it dream in peace beneath its counterpane.

High Noon

Golden, and little bigger than a toy balloon,
Floats on the arch of curving day.
The sky is falling half away,
    And soon
Will lift aloft a dim and shadow-grey
    Low moon.

Rising Rain

By noon a shrouded sun appears.
    Slowly the day's face clears,
And as the wet road glints and gleams
    The surface steams.
I stand there, slipping off my mack
And watch the drizzle drifting back.

The Path Ahead

Over a stile
I saw a path go, so I followed it.
At first we beat about the bush a bit,
But in another mile
My path had struggled steeply to the ridge,
Run raggedly across it through the gorse,
Seen where the wide green valley had a bridge
Across the winding of a water course,
And could not calmly sit,
But headlong like a rolling carpet sped
Down to the river bed.
I let it go ahead,
And saw the sun come out, the winding water lit.

Failing Orator

Sound as a bell he was in wind and lung.
The people hung
Upon his brazen tongue,
And with his pealing period's roll
They swayed, they swung.
But time in turn has taken toll:
Changes are being rung.

Point of Tears

Sky-holding hills across the bay are plain:
A sign of rain,
As eyes grow brighter when a salting tear
Is ominously near.
Later, the hills are gone. The sky is free -
Falling, falling into the salt sea.

Return Journey

Across this countryside
I used to walk with youth's impatient stride,
Seeking as far abroad as footpaths find,
With time ahead to leave long hours behind.
Now, in my ancient days,
I scan far hilltops through a summer haze,
Telling where landmarks hide,
Calling on lanes and paths to come their ways,
Bringing them back to mind.
And sometimes, when the air is very clear,
They do come near.

Pulsar

The dead of summer night, and yet no death,
Only the wide land, lying in the dark,
Holding its breath,
Listens, to mark
Beyond the pale of silence fallen far,
The faint pulsation of a secret star.

Taking Off

The road to base was long but now we're there.
Bowed bodies turn, ease off the crushing pack.
Our arms hang limp
And long and loosely, like a chimp,
Whereas our back,
Let slack,
Rises up inches in the air.
It only feels that way, or wouldn't people stare!

Fixed Pattern

If we could only work the thread afresh
Ripping a life undone
Where fallen stitches run
Through patterns ill repeated :- But its mesh
That followed false directions from our prime,
Is ravelled into time,
Caught till the casting off of mortal flesh.

Monster Calm

High water, liquid glass:
No sail can pass
On this suspended scene.
Here, on a baking beach, between
Bare groynes that dip
Below the glaze of bottle-green,
Deep in its molten mass,
There is no now - it all has been;
Until the heavy waters lean
Forward a little, slip,
And bite the pebbles with a glassy lip.

Initial Effort

Ten men went to mow,
Went to mow a meadow.
Three of these, and other three
Were see bee eye and tea, you see,
And three were little Neddo.
Standing by was icy eye
Who owned the blooming meadow.

Frost

Frost pinches leaf
And shrivels shoot
And blights the blossomed
Hope of fruit.
Under the hill
Is frozen death.
There is no breath
Beneath an icy moon, in staring, starlit still.

Sea Moon

The sea moon sheds a fishy skin
Across the waters, casting in
Her shoal of silver scale,
And rises, cold and pale.
Against the starry sieve of night
Her naked stare is bold and hard,
But from her sea-way, lunar starred,
She looks in liquid light.

Fugitive Flints

When sun and rounded moon together pull
The sea-bed full,
High waters, racing on a Channel run,
Fall on the flank where Downs are deep
And scour below the soaring sweep
That looks to stand till all is done,
Remote, as if asleep;
While on the cliff-top, one by one,
Soft-bonded flints, sharp shifting stone,
Crop out from under, creep
To stare beneath the moon, and lie there in the sun.

Golden Sovereign

Darkness is first to fall,
Soon as the golden disc, that was a ball,
Has dropped beyond the sharpened edge of day,
        Draining the hillside grey.
        Darkness, the first to fall,
Takes down the young, the weak, the small,
As lark lies low and swallows skim away.
        Then all the lamps of town
        Cast their long shadows down
        And light of sprinkled star
Is shed from long ago and very far.
Night goes to earth, and all across the land,
Drawn by her stealthy hand,
Frail sleepers fall, like leaves, and as they drop,
        For each descending one
The darkened world comes spinning to a stop.
But all the while, the golden spending sun
        Sinks down, in slotted slide,
And when it rises, on the morning side,
        Still flat and very wide,
The earth goes round again, the people stand.

On Preparing a Pigeon

It had some twenty acorns in its crop.
None of your 'Peel and grate or finely chop',
                Just, glop!
You happy birds of feather
With gullets made of leather!
You lucky school of fins and tails
That have no kitchen round your scales!
Oh, fortunate you folk of fur
That never need to stand and stir!
Pity our poor degenerate craw
Too feeble to digest you raw.

Olympic Flame

The fire's fallen dead
With the logs lying bare,
Yet, forcefully fed
By the blast of the bellows,
A flimmering flare,
The palest of yellows,
Is lured from its lair
All alone.

Peering and peeping
It's easy to scare
Like all its frail fellows
Who come up for air.
They sally and gutter
And furtively flutter
Or dally and dither
And rally and slither,
Yet, cautiously creeping,
Are daring to dare
The unknown.

Now heat that lay sleeping
Is suddenly there
And the flames have gone spare:
They are blazing and bold,
Swirling and sweeping
And larrupping, leaping,
They've flown!

And filled with their flowing
The hearth is aflame.
It's a glorious game
Now the heat's taken hold,
And they're glowing
And going for gold.

Desolation

A sole survivor soldiers on,
The last one left to grieve,
All that was loved is dead and gone:
No hopes to build, no ties to bind.
Living and loving left behind
And nothing to retrieve;
A time of drought, of dearth and lack,
No shoulder, firm to lean upon,
No future path, no turning back,
No fond farewells, no goods to pack:
A life is due to leave.

Mates

When you and I stood on the stack,
And you without your shirt,
You used to say, Just scratch my back.
It itched from straw and dusty dirt.
I scratched it till it must have hurt.

When summer pastures drone with flies
And bunching cattle wait,
With crusted insect round their eyes,
They stand or lie beside a mate.
Each puts its head to other's tail
And beats the flies off with its flail.

When both our days are getting late
And all desires fail,
I shall still lie beside my mate,
- of course, not head to tail! -
And scarify around the spine
Which I regard as partly mine.

New Inspiration

Clearing the rock of winter's block
A trickle welling out
Streaks in the sand of drought
Where sudden seedlings sprout.
And now comes down a flock
Of birds, and herds of thirsty words
Are wondering about.

No Light

I sleep with the dark,
Secure until dawn.
The light may not enter:
Our curtains are drawn.

Ah, love of my heart,
I am nobody's wife
Now the one point of light
Has gone out of my life.

The moon may be risen,
The stars all aspark;
I make me this prison
To weep with the dark.

Marriage

Their marriage knew consuming flame
When even nostrils flare.
At last a calmer radiance came,
But all the warmth was there;
And now, to keep their joy the same,
They make it their affair.

Miller, Still Jolly

Since I am little good to beast
And none at all to man,
And creep where once I ran,
And take up little room,
Now let it be my care, at least,
Not to go out in gloom.
For us about to be deceased
Expectancy is not increased
By sight of lawyer, doctor, priest;
And if beyond the tomb
I find another living span,
Just as my rising life began
From out my mother's womb,
They tell me it will be a feast.
I'll taste it - if I can.

Why Cry?

Pretended it was onions, but I knew
Better. Besides, there was no onion smell.
My nose can always tell,
And hers was slightly red. Another clue:
Her glasses all askew.
I said straight out I knew that was a lie.
It wasn't onions got her in a stew.
She said, 'Those thousands murdered! War is hell.'
I thought, one doesn't cry
When foreign strangers die.
A lovers' tiff, I thought. I took a pew
And tried to cheer her up. I do it well,
I'm tactful. If I don't succeed, I try
To find a basic cause, discover why.

Ancient Chimney

Under the mantel-tree, where night meets day,
The hearth is dead:
Yet breath of ashes, stirring with the wind's lift,
Draws the last gasp of grey
To drift
Up the chimney cavern. Here long loping flames
Leapt through their flickering of life, and fled
- Golden and ruddy red -
To darkness gaping overhead;
Funnelled as phantoms through the feathered black
Of the soft-sooted stack
With its wide, ancient aperture, which frames
A distant, fading star,
Still burning, infinitely far.

Beachy Head

Beyond the cliff-top edge,
Below the wheeling, screaming of the gulls,
The chasm pulls.
Before you leap
And land all broken on a broken ledge,
Look! See how utterly remote they are,
So dwindled down, so small,
Those slow, unceasing waves that creep
Across the shrunken shore, and crawl
Backwards in slower motion, dragging on the rocks.
There you will leave no scar;
There moves indifference no reeling horror shocks.
Time passes to and from upon a tide
That seems eternal, yet can never bide
Nor care, nor cast a glance aside
To tell who fell so far.
And look! Behind, the world is open, wide.

Self-knowledge

Henceforth I'll try
Not to deceive myself; for who would lie
And lose a life-long friend thereby?
Deception must
Bring gullibility or sad mistrust.
Surely I know and love me far too well
Ever to tell
Lies to a liar. Whether heaven or hell
Exist, there is no telling, so I just
Hope to make purer ashes, finer dust.

Down and Out

A steady rain upon his coat
Is drumming out a warning note.
It means to saturate him through:
Coat, jersey, shirt and trousers too;
Then stealing cold against his skin
And foiled from seeping further in,
To trickle down and fill his shoe.
If he could only have a roof
Comparatively waterproof
Like people who are home and dry
Conceivably he need not die.

Identity

The grass is green beyond the fence,
A distance beckons blue.
I'll stir my stumps and get me hence
To see if it is true
That *Where* has but a changing sense,
Unalterable, *Who.*

White Eagle, Roused from the Death Sleep

(viewing his first television programme
with apologies to Hiawatha)

Warm it was within the wigwam,
Darkness lay upon the daytime,
For the flap was fastened over.
Old Nokomis, Chief White Eagle,
Laughing Stock and their papooses,
There they sat before the See-set,
Sat and watched the strange Puk-Wudjies,
Little people, sly enchanters,
Watched until their eyes grew heavy
Very sound asleep the chief was;
Dropped his far-see bread and meat-clasp;
While the white teeth of his children
Ceased to churn their Gitche Gumee.
Then his wife rose up lamenting:
'Wahnonomin' - So she woke him.
'Home you brought the Little People
On the terms of keep or render;
Go and take them back White Eagle
Fear them, for they conquered Kwasind.'
'Ugh,' they answered all and each one.

(Kwasind - as any serious student knows- was lulled to sleep and killed by the Puk-Wudjies.)

The Wish

The frame a little buckled, slightly bent
No longer spry
Can go no longer where it always went;
But when the mind is gone, its power spent,
Then let the body die.

The Kindling

He always showed a face of stone
And kept his thoughts his very own.
        His eye was hard as flint.
        Then, by some saving grace,
        Somebody struck a spark,
And out there sprang across the dark
        Stone face
        A sudden glint.

The Search

Yes, cleanliness was next, but work was God.
It was his living bread, his reason, hope,
        His life's connecting-rod;
Kept him, moreover, always neatly shod
        And regularly paid his rent.
But now redundant hands can only grope,
And men stood off take feet that plod
        Over the same old ground
In search of something that may not be found
        And is not easy to invent.

Reluctant Rising

First light insinuates a stealthy day.
Darkness, diluted thinly drains away
Beyond the waiting walls, soon solid, set.
        Time to get up. Not yet!
        But light is there,
Laying the day's directive out to air.
It clearly came to strip the bed, and hovers,
        Itching to pluck the covers.

Wasting Winter

Now that winter's on the move
    - Long overdue -
As the celandine can prove,
    Sun-painted new,
Off he shuffles, bending low.
    See his livid hue,
Mark his movements, numb and slow
    Feel a little rue.
    Old folk are few
That may live their part and go
    Dead on cue.

Skylark

His call comes from the blue, and draws the eye
Up to the very vault of summer sky
To catch that quivering of ecstasy:
A winging joy that floods the sky and spills
Sweet sprinkle far below on plunging hills.
  Syrinx of summer air,
  Shrill pipe, of Pan possessed,
He soars beyond the bounds of earthly care;
Yet, when his wings cry out at last for rest,
He guards the secret of his grassy nest
  And will not plummet there.

Passing Fair

A castle built by children's hand
And spade and bucket, out of sand,
Melts to a mound and swirls away.
Such early lessons, learned in play
Work for the world's entire endeavour:
Transience, made to last for ever.

Summer Holidays

Salt smell of serried stone
Baking on sunlit beach
Or damply nobbled underneath the prone
Shivering swimmer's leach;
Whiteness of cliff and gulls, grey wheeling screech;
Dapple of sun on water, dazzles flown
From darting eye's bewildered reach;
All this, and warmth that seeps into the bone:
Long summer days with nobody to teach!

So Here We Come Then

Here we come gathering our may,
Frosty bloom along the thorn.
Summer comes to pull away
Petals from the flowering spray
Where the crimson berry's borne.
Nuts are nothing, here and now:
Nuts go hang on autumn's bough!
Through the fickle changing year
Berries hang on hope and fear,
Hanging over hopes of hay,
Over cares of cropping corn.
Nuts may ripen, fruit may fall,
Nuts may never come at all.
Nuts are neither here nor there -
Everything is in the air,
Nothing for certain, everything is May.
So here we come then, gathering our day.

Snow

I thought the sky must fall, and when it did
        All sky and air were one:
A swirl of staring stars in slow descent
Upon the muffled land; still lying, white and spent
        When morning brought the sun.
Now that the sky was down, the blue air went
Endlessly upward, but the earth lay huddled, hid.

Old Moon

Give me the curded moon with horny rind,
        Or let me trace
The shadows of an old enchanted face
Beyond a frosted window, lantern-shined.
        Give me to find
The slender bow of bright Diana's chase,
Or sight a glinting sickle, sharp-defined,
With stars for harvesting and spells to bind;
And let there be a murrain on mankind,
        Proud in that place,
Plundering moonstones that had shone in space
        Time out of mind.

March Promise

March is not always wild: it has its days
        - A mad moon's lucid phase -
When morning wears a calm unclouded brow.
The soaring sky sheds in a radiant haze
A sifted bloom on land as green as grape,
And the still trees, laid bare in wintry shape,
Are pale with promise haunting on the bough:
The wraith of shrouded Aprils, long forgotten Mays.

Summer's Going

Now swallows in successive waves
Will score their music on the staves
That stretch from pole to pole:
A neat notation on the wire
From each contributory choir
For one concerted whole.
On lines we drew against the sky
To speak from A to Zed
They set their music, very high,
And far above our head,
In soaring, transcendental clef
To which our mortal ear is deaf,
Our mortal heart is dead.
A thousand thousand living notes
With music pouring from their throats
Come swooping down from John O'Groats,
Each taking up the thread.
Minim and crochet perch abreast
Where once a bar denoted rest
When earlier notes had sped.

A sudden little semibreve
Sings out a signal, and they leave.

Straight Trees

So many sturdy trees, long standing,
Affirmatively reaching for the light,
Soon felled, hauled away to the landing,
Sold down the river, bought up by the Press,
            Smashed to a pulpy mess,
And by a long-established right
            Deliberately slanted.

Purr

To make so soft a sawing note
Consistently occur
Some rotor in her velvet throat
Is surely lined with fur.
Are buttered cogwheels going round
With rumble of recurrent sound?
I asked her if they were.
Her look was languidly remote,
And still she did not stir.
Your average contented mog
Has no conception of a cog:
The origins of purr
Are all the same to her.

Old Couple

When love is sturdy grown and fledged to leaf
    Its flower holds the seed
    - Long shaping, slowly set -
Of suffering. I could be happy yet
    But that I know,
However long the ripening, and slow,
    All flowers grow
To death. It is God's will and nature's need
    That joy must come to grief.

Posters

I am always amazed at the zest
Of the people who poster their chest.
The pectoral logo
For me is a no-go.
I won't let you write on my vest.

Waiting Room

Four rows of chairs; an old man with a stick;
Family group: the boy looks very sick;
A weighty woman with asthmatic breath;
                    A clock, no tick.
              All waiting time is slow,
But now it will be over. I shall know.
Then if the sentence be not life, but death,
Leaving this building I shall still be quick

The Martyr

One bound by honour to a martyr's stake
Suffered for conscience sake
Hoping to rise a phoenix from the fire,
To kindle and inspire.
Martyrs are many, over all the earth,
Dead from disease and dearth
Or dying suicidal for a cause
Against despotic laws
Of modern Ghengis Kahn or Tamburlaine.

The Players

Each was the other's answer to the *Why*
              Of being
Less than a flicker in the eye
              Of the All-seeing.
In this as in all fair exchange agreeing
They played along together, passed the buck;
              But it was just their luck
That one be left to hold it, and the other die.

Population Control

When first two cells emerged from one,
Was reproduction any fun?
Who was the father, who the son?
Was it deliberately done?
And when they further subdivided,
Were they omnisciently guided
Not to resolve, as you and I did,
That lest the world be overrun
We two would always stay as one?

Riddled Sky

Along the forest ridge, across the Weald,
Small flocks of random-perching people live.
Their lamps, lit lonely, pointed fine and pale,
        Pin down the dark, and nail
Their nighted hillside to that rising field
Where studded stars, struck from beyond the dark,
        Prick through, with scattered spark,
And hang as asterisks, perhaps to give
Some little glim, but nothing clear revealed.

Sad Case

How far declined are we who live,
        How absolutely ablative!
All moving down to having been,
        Longing to mean
Something that might not pass beyond recall
As Spring pricks out the shape of Autumn's fall
And Winter stares at Summer in between.

With Heavy Heart

They took the body of my lover, dead,
But still his heavy head
Leans as in life against my heart
So that we never move apart.
I will take heart, my love; there's much to do.
I will not die, but live, and live for two.

Transplants

I used to be a man of many parts,
But shed a few in passing - lost some hair
And nearly all my teeth; went short on sight;
But had the new parts fitted, and with care
    I can still bite,
    Still stare.
But now's the time disintegration starts,
    When wear begins to tear.
Soon I shall need to have a big repair.
And though they do replacement jobs with hearts,
My body's obsolete. I'll do without.
    Too old to travel on a spare,
    I shall decide I've done my share,
Tick myself off and quietly clock out.

The Way In

They took the thin end of the wedge
And stuck it underneath the edge.
Soon, with a little cautious prising,
It looked as if the lid was rising;
Till those who stood around to scoff
Were shocked to find the lid was off.

Sharp Showers

An April shower, on the run,
Hotly pursued by blazing sun,
        Came down upon the roof
and finding it was waterproof
        Slid down the slates
            On skates,
        Dropped from the eaves,
Swam swiftly down a small canal
Through feathers, moss and leaves
            Et al,
        Fell down a spout,
            Shot out
And quietly went into the underground;
While the beleaguered sun soon found
Fresh glinting rain blades closing in around.

The Paddling Pier

What giant bucket, what enormous spade
Dug the foundations when our pier was made?
As its first sea-leg took a step from land
And sank a firming foot below the sand,
Was there a cheer,
A cry, God bless our pier!
From awed spectators on Marine Parade,
Wondering how far out those feet might wade?
Such creatures came to live on all our shores,
Not on all fours,
But stalking tall to seaward, many-legged,
With feet well driven down, securely pegged.
Poor centipede!
Forever captive, never to be freed!

It put a blight on
His hope of trips to Hastings and to Brighton.
Small boats swam by, big steamers made their landing,
Hooted, broke free, swanned off and left him standing.
No, not for him
A chance to join the bathers in a swim,
His fettered legs by iron bars bestraddled.

Resigned, he hitched his girders up, and paddled.

Trailing Clouds, Gory

He was a *Family* butcher, and my young heart used to clop
Like horses' hooves whenever mother went into his shop.
        I knew that she was brave and strong,
        I knew I often got things wrong.
        She never took her child along
            But left me in the street.
        Did I, perhaps, look tender meat?
        I used to stand and feel the shock
        Of hatchet on the chopping block
        And see the sawdust by the door
        Bestrewn with little specks of gore.
Once, in the street, he stopped to pat my head,
Draining my cheeks of all their healthy red.
        I fled.
Young minds are clouded with primaeval dread,
        Although no word of it is said.

Winter Pattern

Now feathers quill
And weather's chill,
And scant the pickings on the hill,
        And so
The silent song birds go
To beg their fill
On step and sill
By quilted lawns below;
And where the snow
Lies smooth and still
        They sew
Spickly their threaded tacks with pricking toe.

Tilted Clock

A day is just emerging, duly stamped
        With proper name and date.
Only the kitchen clock is hanging late,
Limping, a tock grown longer than a tick.
This new arrangement, hastily revamped,
Sends on the seconds with a glancing gait,
        Waiting at slow for quick.
But time is not for us to syncopate,
Though passing hours may seem extended, cramped.
        No cheating time or tide!
They swing remorselessly from side to side,
Wound by an ancient Day's imponderable weight.

Through a Glass

Upon reflection,
Holding the mirror in a better light,
He saw surprising imperfection,
And sideburns undergrown with white.
And further on reflection
He saw the world was all the wrong way round
And though the thought was not profound
He put aside the mirrored sight
In deepening dejection.

Hunger Eats the Seed

He never learnt to count or write or read,
But calculate he can
His likely living-span
From knowledge born of unremitting need,
By rote of endless toil
In long-eroded soil
Where seasons fail and hunger eats the seed.
This quickening of breath
Will soon be put to death:
Small starving scion of a dying breed.

Unseasonable Comment from Mother Christmas

Every Christmas, never fail,
We get a crop of begging mail.
There's one thing does annoy me rather,
That all the letters come to Father.
In all my years of working hard
I've never had a Christmas card.
Who feeds our stock, do you suppose,
While Nick goes off to reindeer shows?
And when he services the sleigh,
Who is it puts his tools away?
Who helps with mucking out the stables,
Ties up the parcels, licks the labels?
Sometimes, when wrapping up a gift,
I tend to feel a little miffed:
So much to do, I've never even
Made it to the Feast of Stephen;
And after Christmas, hard to bear,
There's all that sooty underwear.
Don't talk to me of Christmas cheer -
This year I've had it up to here.
If no-one cares that I exit
I may end up a feminist.

Flicker Flattery

A green stick, supple, newly sawn,
Is carried to the hearth and flung
Across the blazing seasoned, brittle
        Brown.
Then licking flames that lap and fawn
Fall on the green with forking tongue,
Flicker it, flatter it, lick-sap-spittle
        Down
To ashes fallen grey with ashy dawn.

Confrontation

A plump Arachnid, black as ink,
Had come to drink
By darkness at a water hole
Down at the bottom of a sink.
Safe on a rope of homespun thread,
He reached his goal.
Then, thirst assuaged, he saw with dread
There was no hanging silver chain;
To help him clamber up again;
So, yearning for the missing link,
He settled down to have a think
And thought and thought, but all in vain,
Beside an upturned washing bowl.

At dawning light's first early chink
- (the spider hadn't slept a wink) -
A monster crawled from out of bed,
And soon its frightful hairy head,
Its noxious nose, a shocking pink,
Voracious mouth, all white and red,
Rose high above the valley's brink.
A plug swung down to fill the drain,
A fleshy feeler moved the bowl.
    Nothing was said.
Then came a shriek to wake the dead:
    The monster fled.

As for the upward-swarming spider,
He thought he was the terrifyder.

The Owl's Tale

I wonder, sir, if I might make so bold
As just to step inside out of the cold?
The speaker was no nightingale, no chiff-chaff:
A humble passerine, mere avian riff-raff,
To wit, a sparrow. Yet I let him in
And laced his grain with just a spot of gin.
We owls are far too wise to set a tray
Of dainties out for cats to take away,
But if some humble bird hops to our table,
    As well as we are able,
Without a lot of snobbish fuss
    We make him one of us.
    The same with mice:
All plebs, but when you get to know them, nice.

My barn is roomy, all the world was white.
I offered him a shakedown for the night
And he accepted it, as well he might.
The Christmas truce was on, and I was tight.
Insomniacs will often rise to eat:
It helps them sleep when next they hit the sheet.
I could not sleep, so moved around a bit
- And found my guest had done a moonlight flit!
That gin had worked through to the frozen marrow
Of a peculiarly astute young sparrow.
    It made me feel an awful twit.
I'm wise now - if your guest is eatable
Be sudden rather than hospitable.

(Based on the Christmas story when animals observe a truce of not preying on each other.)

Dawn in a Garden

So early in the morning, utter still:
That gap beyond the clock's arrested tick.
Nothing occurs,
Steeped in a magic chill,
Without a sound or any motion, till
Some exhalation from the sleeping ground
Makes petals tremble. Then a song-bird stirs
And feathers flutter, flick;
And in a while the waking air is quick
With shrill and strident sound.
A bank of cloud has built behind the hill.
The morning's getting up, the wind soon will.

Maturity

When we are very nearly dead
From age or from disease
There grows a new awareness
Of little things that please,
The milk of human kindness
Is not the least of these

Company

When introduced to so and so
I'm none too sure I care to know
My smile is sweet, my tone is bright
And conversation's most polite.
But when I'm home beside my love
And giving his arm a friendly shove
There's not much conversation heard
Sometimes we hardly say a word.

The Chasm

I walked up to the generation gap,
Tried to communicate across the chasm;
Made out some flowing-hairy sort of chap
And thought, Some mother has 'em!

He looked across at me. Now, did he think
God! that old blighter must be on the blink?
We stood and stared across the great divide:
His hair so long, mine short at back and side.

Apprehension

He takes things as they come: I go to meet
Halfway the shape of trouble still in store,
    To fend it off before
It falls upon my neck or round my feet.
I must confront it, never let it loom
Longer and larger, stalking down the street.
    Worse troubles then at sea?
Peer from the window, hurry through the door . . .
It changes shape. Returning in defeat
    I find it in my room:
Let itself in. Most troubles have my key.
Sits there like frozen snow that waits for more.

The Catalyst

If I had not there would have been
No wild recriminating scene
With passion boiling hot.
Such fishy kettles stew for years
And nothing untoward occurs
Until a meddling finger stirs
What simmered in the pot,
So decorously hid.
If I had known what soon I knew
I should have left their juice to stew:
A pretty kettle, full of fish!
I never should have touched the lid,
But did.
Oh, now I wish, Oh, how I wish
And wish that I had not.

Fogbound

Beyond the railings of Marine Parade
    All sea and sky are one
    Under a smothered sun.
The sky came shrouding on the tide and stayed
To wall the sea behind a blank facade.
The water slumbers, silent - calm, not tame -
    And plays a waiting game,
Sleeping to turn of tide, when sea-wind stirs
    And sets its sinews free.
Only the foghorn wakes, despairing, slurs,
    And slumps into the sea.

Squirrels

Ragtail and Bobtail have no pedigree -
You'd never get far up their family tree.
    They climb among cobnuts,
    The most highly rated,
    The terribly snob nuts,
    The most cultivated.
    Alas for all posh nuts!
    They seem to be fated
    To end up as nosh nuts
    And get hibernated
In Ragtail and Bobtail, the wild and the free,
Who like to climb up in their family tree.

Noise

Sound travels straight, but noise goes round the bend
And drives us with it. Silence is a friend
That never comes to stay - until the end.

Dandelion Time

No putting back the clock: the seeded hours
Trailing a downy-silken parachute,
Drop on the sea - flats where the salt winds scours
    Or waft upon a stillness, drift
Below a sheltered bank, to strike a root
That taps, by taper deep and hard to shift,
In summers far ahead, with circled golden flowers.
And frailty bearing up the dying fruit.

Groynes

Groynes go ranking down the beach
And hold the shingle in their raking reach.
        They keep
Steady the foreshore on its eastern creep,
    Stemming the tidal flow.
        They breach
The Channel roller in its breaking leap
    And staunch its underflow.
    And when the tide is low,
Down to the sands their cockled girders go,
To firm the curving shore in one serrated sweep.

Seagulls

We watched the seagulls wheel,
Sinewed to sweep and soar
And slew at feathers' feel
    Where currents bore.
We watched them on the sand.
Steady and still they stand
    Beaks to the wind,
To keep their feathers pinned.

Guidance

I asked my soul (if any) what was good
In action. He at last replied (if there)
'Refrain from doing harm,' as if you could
Whose breath infects the air!
This counsel (if it was) - of calm despair
Provided (if anything) a rough and ready rood.

Hardly Fair

Nothing had asked to be, all were shanghaied
        To live until they died.
Some might have wished to hear the pros and cons
        Before they took it on
Once here we find there's no alternative
        But eat to live.
It's hardly fair that tiger eats gazelle
        But what the hell?
The tiger's hungry, has an appetite.
        Ask the gazelle if that's all right.
He makes no answer, being now digested,
        Tiger invested.
Now ask - Homo Sapiens.

Stopgaps

Just for the record, play that thing once more:
Birth, apprehension, growing awareness, death:
Breathing, struggle to keep on breathing, end of breath
        And off the air.
I think I know now what we're playing for;
    Know why, in echoed sound,
We are continually going 'round,
Making a repetitious, hollow chime:
    Strains
No erudite Musician helpfully explains.
His programme has a little space to spare.
    - We fill up time.

Natural Injustice

Nature has no conception of the just,
Her law enforced by talon, tooth and beak.
The hungry tiger strikes because he must;
A roebuck falls. No God protects the weak.

Man has invented justice, to ignore it
Wherever power and influence prevail;
Made wigs and woolsacks, docks and benches for it,
Kept it secure with gibbet and with gaol.

Our greed is paramount, our wealth is flaunted,
The hungry bear a stigma, take the blame.
The sadness of our centuries is haunted
By ghosts lamenting their rejected claim.

Nature is careless, callous, wanton, wild.
Unjust humanity is nature's child.

Bystanders

I cannot take that manger in the cold,
The saviour's birth, by angel voice foretold,
The legendary shepherds on their knees,
The kings with myrrh and frankincense and gold
I can take none of these.
But the dull cattle, with their lowing tongue,
Theirs is an anthem sung
Beyond belief, a humble, earthy sound.
I put myself along
Those stolid beasts. We simply stand around.

Violence

People in glasshouses shouldn't throw stones,
People with skeletons shouldn't break bones.
If you agree that society's sick
You won't bring its heart up by heaving a brick.

Pop Star

Those celebrated Sirens of the past
Who turned unhappy sailors into swine
Or gloated over rocks where ships were cast,
Singing on hilltops far above the Rhine
    Dirges of dire despair
- Those faded females are fast losing heart,
Outnumbered by their modern counterpart,
    Most often male,
Whose strains enjoy the freedom of the air.
His singing doesn't match the Lorelei
    - It does not rise so high -
And as he sends across his soulful wail
He isn't sitting in a garment scanty
    Facing a gale.
Thousands of young and clamorous Bacchante
Fight for admission to his lurid lair
To glean the combings of his golden hair,
He has his fill of victims, and to spare.

But if it's any consolation, Circe,
His victims also have him at their mercy.

Discouragement

I ask you, what's the good?
You'd better tell me, if you could;
But say, reproachful, sad,
Despairing? Ah, that's bad.

To Stodger

I sing to Stodger of the copper bottom,
Staunch servitor who fifty years has been
My safe-environmental wash-machine.
No gold can buy his like: no shop has got 'em.

Who has not marvelled as they see him stodging?
Driving fresh air th'opposèd holes between,
Sluicing those suds which make all garments clean,
Sucking and swirling where the dirt is lodging.

Mine is the shoulders' and the elbows' toil,
His art restores the White its pure serene
And keeps all Colours true, yet still most green,
For weary waters sleep in garden soil.

Wizard of washday, hear my plea devout:
Sweet Stodger, still be stalwart, see me out.

Nature Trail

Only the tail
Showed it had been a squirrel. Nothing swerved or slowed;
The body gone, one with the bloody road.
If all accumulated killing showed,
This surface would be bristling with the trail
Of hedgehogs; tarred with fur and feather, tooth and nail,
Fingers of mole, crushed head of harmless toad.
Then surely none could fail
To stop and think, and think in terms of war,
With no memorial, no recorded scar,
But slaughter almost on a human scale.

Picker Pest

That picker with her greedy bowl
Is prowling in my canes,
Not yet content with all she stole
And seeking what remains.
No cure for picker pest is known.
I rise at dawn for Peck Your Own:
We birds can't lie abed.
Then pickers come to take their toll:
A garden pest beyond control
While raspberries are red.

Ham

Who said the time is out of joint
- Said it and felt it?
Who said it's time the joint was out?
I did - I smelt it.

View from a Hill

When we are young we sometimes climb a hill,
Arrive exultant, look down from on high
And feel that much is plain;
But if we turn and lie
Face upward, still,
And see how much is sky,
We sometimes think again.

Abdication

If I'm to be Queen of the May, mother
I'll have to be scantily gowned
So hear what the weather men say, mother
I don't really want to get drowned.
If cloudy the outlook and grey, mother
When I'll just be sitting around
I'll give all my garlands away, mother
I don't think I care to be crowned.

The Grain

Please do not put me on a list:
I am not any kind of -ist
Only a tiny grain of sand
Which something inconceived has planned
Inside a seething sea.
I'm going round and round and round
And grinding down and being ground
And all will go against the grain
Till nothing of it shall remain
That was the likes of me.

Index of First Lines